$16.95

791.43   Guttmacher, Peter.
GUT 4/98   Legendary sci-fi
        movies

LEGENDARY SCI-FI MOVIES

LEGENDARY SCI-FI MOVIES

Peter Guttmacher

MetroBooks

MetroBooks

An Imprint of Friedman/Fairfax Publishers

DS

© 1997 by Michael Friedman Publishing Group, Inc.

Library of Congress Cataloging-in-Publication Data

Guttmacher, Peter.
  Legendary sci-fi movies/ Peter Guttmacher.
      p. cm.
  Includes bibliographical references and index.
  ISBN 1-56799-490-3
    1. Science fiction films—History and criticism.   I. Title.
  PN1995.9.S26G88   1997
  791.43'615—dc21   97-7235

Editor: Stephen Slaybaugh
Art Director: Kevin Ullrich
Designer: Galen Smith
Photography Editor: Kathryn Culley
Production Manager: Jeanne Hutter

Color separations by Bright Arts Graphics (S) Pte Ltd
Printed in China by Leefung-Asco Printers Ltd.

1 3 5 7 9 10 8 6 4 2

For bulk purchases and special sales, please contact:
Friedman/Fairfax Publishers
Attention: Sales Department
15 West 26th Street
New York, NY 10010
212/685-6610 FAX 212/685-1307

Visit our website:
http://www.metrobooks.com

ACKNOWLEDGMENTS

The author would like to thank United Planets Commander Stephen Slaybaugh for keeping him in human contact with ground control at all times during the voyage. Intergalactic gratitude also goes to the mad, library scientists at the A.M.P.A.S. Margaret Herrick research facility. Lastly, he telepathically communicates his timeless love and gratitude to she-creature Robin-Rose.

CONTENTS

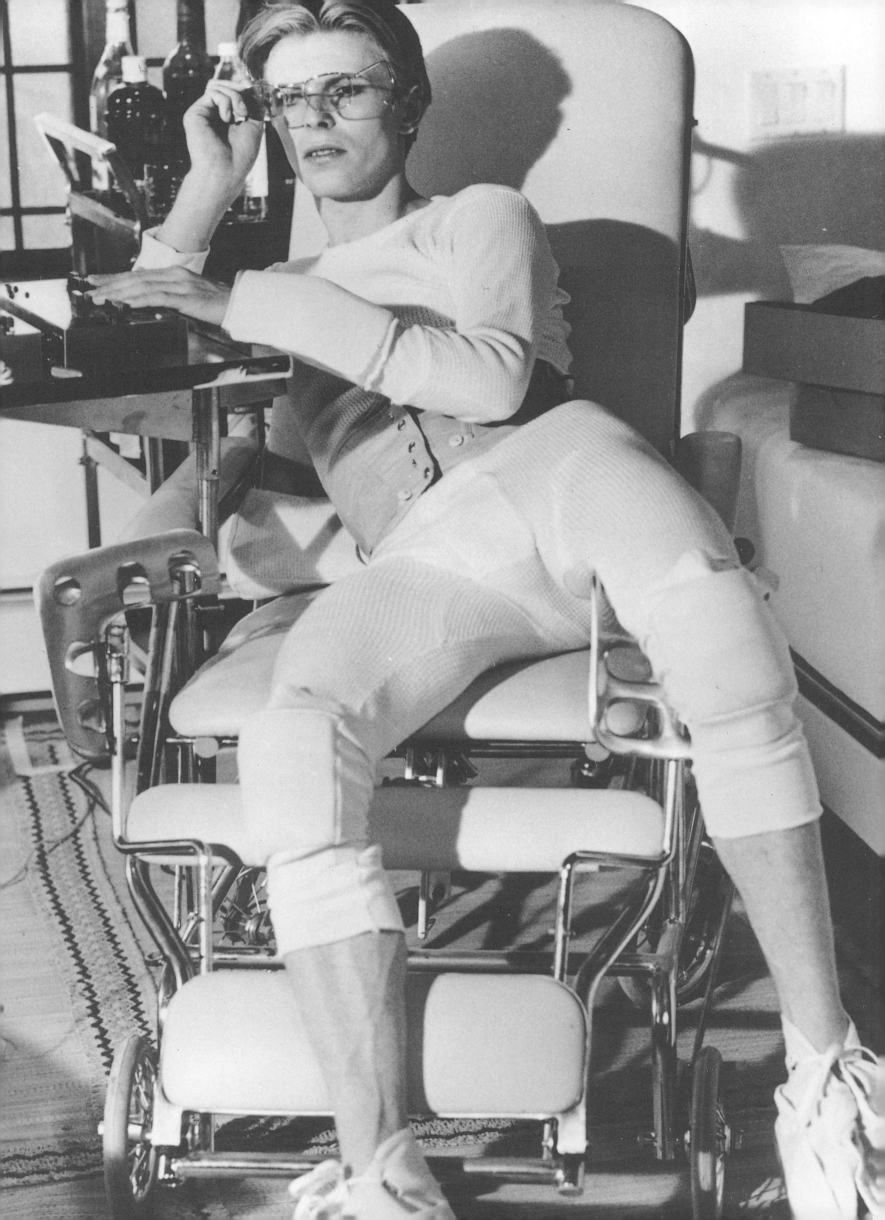

INTRODUCTION

A hundred years from now a book like this will be found only online or on disc because trees will have been declared an endangered species. A hundred years from now a book like this will have been banned and burned by a savagely totalitarian government that finds the book a distraction to the workforce. A hundred years from now we won't need a book like this because we'll be able to telepathically hook up to any information source (thanks to the new technology we'll receive from visiting extraterrestrials). A hundred years from now the sole survivors of the nuclear nightmare will have to travel back in time to read a book like this.

Take your pick. With the genre we've come to affectionately call sci-fi, anything is possible. Ever since 1895, when a certain French illusionist named Georges Méliès first set his imagination's wheels in motion to the speed of the newly invented motion picture camera, the sky (in George's case, the moon) has quite literally been the limit for a filmmaker's fancy. For more than a full century, visionary directors and screenwriters have been taking us to the far reaches of the universe; to the molten center of the earth; deep into the sea's mystery; beyond death; through the barrier of time to meet mutants, monsters, and madmen; onto debased dystopias of terrifying technology; to brave new worlds of intergalactic harmony; and to the holy secrets of the human soul. And all for less than $8.

No film genre can boast as many great writers in its stable, from H.G. Wells to Arthur C. Clarke to Michael Crichton. None other has taken the movie magic of SFX (special effects) to such dizzying heights. Nowhere are there more fanatical fans (just check out a Star Trek convention). And certainly nothing else on the screen has the scope big enough to accommodate boyish Buster Crabbe wearing gold lamé (Flash Gordon: Spaceship to the Unknown, 1936), a hyperintelligent army of irradiated ants in the New

Mexican desert (Them!, 1954), and surgical intelligence acceleration (Charly, 1968).

From westerns (Star Wars, 1977) to horror (Bride of Frankenstein, 1935) to near-documentary (The Andromeda Strain, 1971) to softcore pornography (A Boy and His Dog, 1975) to adventure (Independence Day, 1996) to social commentary (Things to Come, 1936) to metaphysics (A Clockwork Orange, 1971), sci-fi has always made sitting in a dark room the most broadening travel that money can buy, even if it does stop on a Forbidden Planet (1956) or two.

And that's just the sector we're headed for. Make the journey and you'll travel behind the scenes of some of the most celebrated films in sci-fi history. You'll dive back through time (via The Time Machine, 1960, of course) to learn about the literature, pulp magazines, and B serials that made the genre what it is today. You'll confront alien life-forms (like The Thing, 1951) and dissect their biomechanical construction. You'll observe the genesis of little-known gems of the genre (like Chris Marker's La Jetee, 1962, and George Lucas' THX-1138, 1971). You'll voyage to future civilizations (from Fritz Lang's Metropolis, 1926, to Ridley Scott's Blade Runner, 1982) and discover what inspired them. You'll even blow your mind taking the ultimate trip (2001: A Space Odyssey, 1968) and find out just how it was blown.

So, mark your star itinerary for makeup and SFX secrets, and lessons in how to talk like a classic mad scientist or in oh-so-modern Nadsat (the brutal youth of A Clockwork Orange, 1971). Get your life-support systems ready for robotic reviews, alien examinations, and challenging tests in time travel. Set phasers on directorial anecdotes, actors' anguish, and surprising rewrites. We're going where so many have gone before...but never quite like this. 10-9-8-7-6-5-4-3-2-1 Blast off!!!!

OPPOSITE: Ziggy Stardust at the dentist? Guess again. Visiting alien-turned-earth-billionaire Thomas Jerome Newton (David Bowie) puts Howard Hughes to shame, watching twenty television screens at once in Nicolas Roeg's eerily poetic The Man Who Fell to Earth *(1976).*

Chapter One
LEGACY

If I have seen further it is by standing on the shoulders of giants.

—Sir Isaac Newton

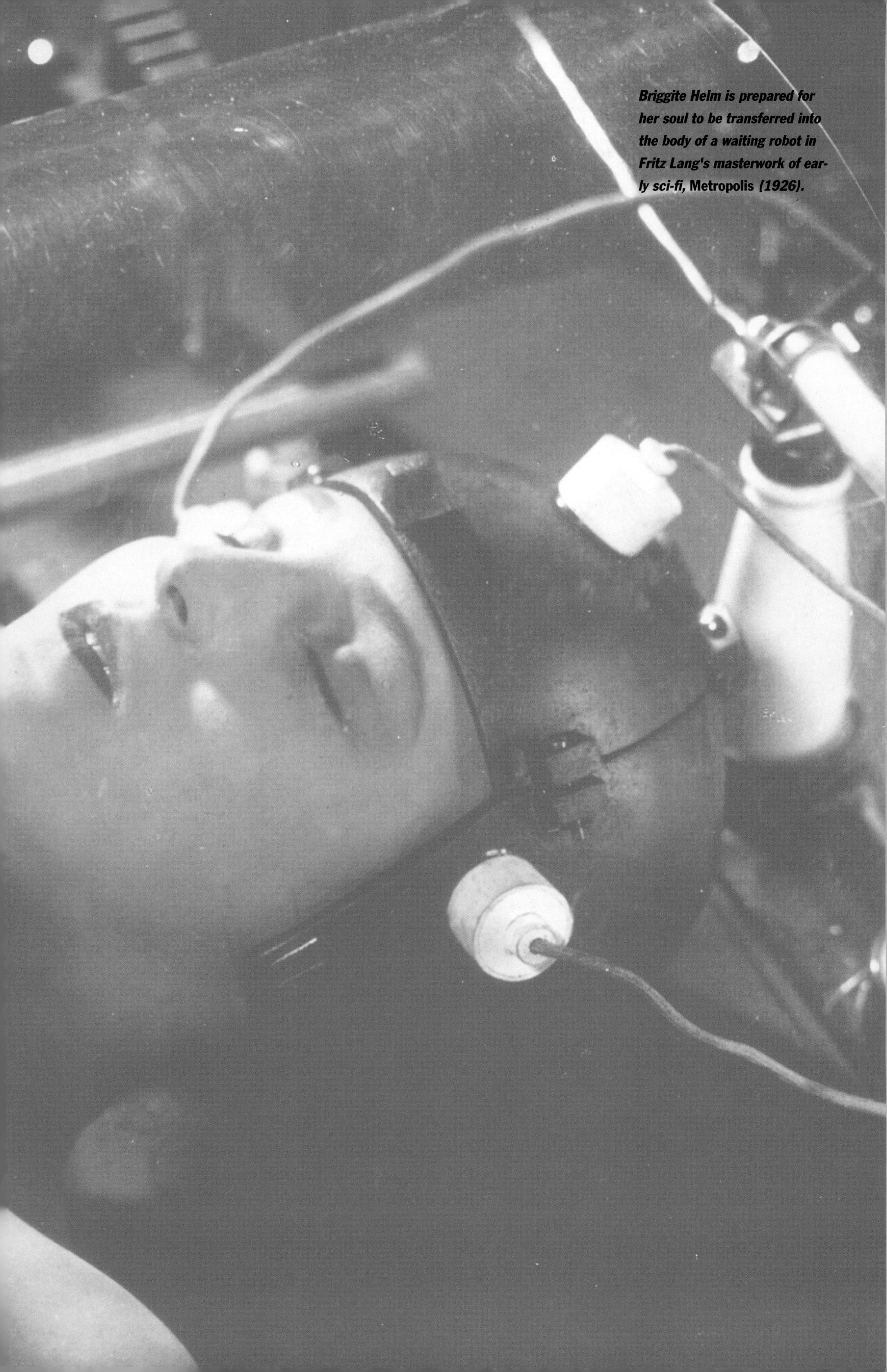

Briggite Helm is prepared for her soul to be transferred into the body of a waiting robot in Fritz Lang's masterwork of early sci-fi, Metropolis *(1926).*

WHEN SCIENCE MET FICTION

Science fiction has always been a natural medium for filmmakers. After all, when you think about it, even the concept of filmmaking sounds scientifically fantastic. Just how far out would the process of recording living images with light, then storing, rearranging, embellishing, and flawlessly projecting them several times their size onto a blank surface have sounded to even the most learned of men during science's infancy? How would the notion of an art form so popular and powerful that it could sway the minds of millions, virtually replacing empirical experience, have struck a struggling Renaissance master? Would entertainment with a price tag boasting

They don't make moon landings like they used to. This famous frame comes from one of sci-fi cinema's first forays, courtesy of French film pioneer George Méliès.

eight zeros have been entertained by the impecunious Bard of Avon? It would have sounded like you had eaten of the mandrake root or been frolicking with the fairies in the moonlight too long. It would have been a one-way ticket to the loony bin or to being burnt at the stake.

Then again, by the end of the nineteenth century the climate was considerably more credulous. As sciences from physics to physiology took their first tentative steps in the laboratory and the field, the Victorian imagination seethed with fancies that only properly repressed Victorian psyches could have come up with.

The scientific and industrial revolution of the 1800s, with its harnessing of the dynamos of electricity and gas combustion, had

brought a whole new bent to speculative fiction. Technology was both tantalizing and terrifying. The same century that saw film's first flickers also saw the first editions of Mary Shelley's *Frankenstein*, Jules Verne's *Twenty Thousand Leagues Under the Sea*, Robert Louis Stevenson's *Dr. Jekyll and Mr. Hyde*, and H.G. Wells' *The Time Machine*. The tremendous popularity of these works of scientific fiction showed that if science was going to become the new god on the block, it needed some serious mythology to attract followers. The public was ripe for a new marvel.

Fittingly enough at the same time, motion pictures were being pioneered by one of the greatest scientists who ever lived. Father of the light bulb, phonograph, telephone, transmitter, quadraplex, and telegraph, Thomas Alva Edison developed his British employee William Kennedy Laurie Dickson's idea of the kinetoscope and kinetograph. The problem was that the viewer had to peer through a hole in a box to watch a twenty- to sixty-second loop of film run in front of a little light bulb. It took France's Lumière Brothers' (Auguste and Louis) 1895 invention of a hand-cranked device for recording longer sections of film and enlarging the images through a motorized projector not unlike those from the old "magic lantern" shows to bring movies to an audience. The Cinematographe was born.

One of France's most ardent admirers of the Cinematographe was thirty-five-year-old illusionist Georges Méliès, who ran Paris' Théâtre Robert-Houdin. In 1896, when the Lumières refused his request to buy their recorded street scenes and slices of Parisian life, he wangled his own equipment from England, and soon projected films became a part of his magic act. Then came a blunder as fortuitous as peanut butter mashing against chocolate. Méliès was screening a film of a carriage when it miraculously transformed itself into a hearse. The fact that his camera had jammed, substituting one image for the other, was not lost on the illusionist. Within weeks audiences were thrilling to *L'Escomptage d'une Dame* (1896) in which a mademoiselle transformed into a skeleton and back again.

These filmed illusions soon gave way to more fanciful filmed stories. Méliès' *La Lune à un Métre* (1898) showed a scientist falling asleep and dreaming about the man in the moon coming through his window. To make the film, Méliès set up the very first film studio in Montreuil, France, complete with glass walls and ceiling (for easier illumination), huge, moving cutouts, and trapdoors for disappearances. He even hand-painted each frame to give his film color.

In 1902 Méliès took the plunge into full-fledged sci-fi, light-hearted though it was, when his appropriately named Star Film Company made the fourteen-minute masterpiece *Le Voyage dans la Lune (Voyage to the Moon)*. Sages whimsically traveled to the moon courtesy of a cannon that shot a bullet-shaped rocket right into the man in the moon's eye. Things weren't much more authentic on the satellite's surface. Scientists without space suits or helmets cavorted with scantily clad moon maidens (ballerinas from the Théâtre du Chatelet). Tumblers from the famed Folies-Bergère fell into craters as volcanos erupted. Umbrellas took root in the lunar soil. And the scientists bravely battled insect-people before heading earthward for accolades from the Académie Française.

From rocket cannons to tribal moon men, scantily clad moon maidens, and equally underdressed astronauts, fantasy reigns supreme in this feast of fantastic images from Méliès' Voyage to the Moon (1902).

Silly? *Mais oui,* but the film was a phenomenal hit. The sci-fi craze was on. Filmmakers worldwide were scrambling to replicate the film. Meanwhile, Méliès had completed more than two hundred short films in less than a decade, pioneering such special effects as multiple exposures, stop-motion, fades, dissolves, split-screen, and even slow and fast motion.

EARLY FLIGHTS OF FANCY AND FEAR

Many turn-of-the-century sci-fi films were...well, let's not mince words, ridiculous. American filmmaker Robert William Paul's *The ? Motorist* (1905) showed a couple speeding so speedily in their roadster that they fly off into outer space, mingle for a while, and return. France's famed Pathé Film Company took viewers on *An Adventure at the Bottom of the Sea* (1906) to watch sea fairies frolic. Britain's *The Motor Valet* (1906) showed a domestic automaton on a rampage that ends with him exploding. France's Segundo de Chomon's *A Trip to Jupiter* (1907) pictured a king climbing an endless ladder through the heavens. The seven-times-remade silent classic *She* (1908) offered a savage queen in darkest Africa with the secret of eternal youth. *A Wonderful Fluid* (1908) made women grow facial hair. *The Man in the Moon Seeks a Wife* (1908) put its title character in a linen suit in a glass bubble. Méliès' own *From Paris to New York by Automobile* (1908) needs no explanation. Whimsy was the word of the day.

The first truly serious sci-fi film, Walter Booth's *The Airship Destroyer* (1909), tapped into both the Wright Brothers' relatively recent feat at Kitty Hawk and H.G. Wells' prophetic novel of aerial bombardment, *The War in the Air*, to spin a story about a young inventor who saves London from Germany's aerial assault by devising a radio-controlled torpedo. As the young century progressed, the tensions leading to World War I gave early sci-fi films a distinctly paranoiac note. Remote-control rays detonated explosives in *Pawns of Mars* (1915). Mental energy was used for the same purpose in *War of Dreams* (1915). Radiation made its victims invisible in *Rays That Erase* (1916).

20,000 Leagues Under the Sea (1916), with its rampaging super-sub, the *Nautilus* (thanks to a one-hundred-foot [30.5m] model and Ernest Williamson's pioneering underwater photography), was released the same week a German U-boat wreaked havoc on New York, sinking a dozen ships. Airships attacked London in *If* (1916) and dirigibles did the same to New York in *Zeppelin Attack* (1917). A sinister machine was put to criminal and lucrative purposes in Hungary's *The Mind Detecting Ray* (1918). Hyperpseudotechnology for a hypertense time.

Enter the white lab coat, the arrogant attitude, and the insane gleam in the eye. Mad scientists were brought cackling into the picture, at first comically, by filmmaking visionary and later director of the celebrated *Napoleon* (1927) Abel Gance, in *La Folie de Docteur Tube* (1915). Doctor Tube, with his wild eyes and bulging brainpan (a result of messing around with light waves), maniacally enjoys shrinking and enlarging animals and people. The innovative Gance made it an eyeful with his use of distorting lenses and mirror effects.

By 1916, the demented doctors were doing what they would do best through sci-fi film history—creating and reviving life itself. Stateside, adapting Owen Davis' play *Lola*, James Young told a tale of a bereaved scientist who brings his daughter back from the dead with an electric ray only to find her malignantly evil in *Without a Soul* (1916). Across the Atlantic in the country that would come to dominate the medium through the remainder of the silent-film era, German filmmaker Otto Rippert did a little creative compiling of his own for his famed *Hommunkulus der Führer* (1916). It was one part Mary Shelley's *Modern Prometheus* (a.k.a. *Frankenstein*), one part Jewish Golem legend of a superman made of clay running amok, and one part seeming forecast of Germany's future two decades down the road. This six-hour serial featured an artificial superhuman created in the lab who, though at first heroic and virtuous, when spurned by his lady love and made aware of his origins turns to evil and destruction. The homunculus becomes the ruthless dictator of his own country and only a thunderbolt from the gods above finally destroys him.

Robert Wiene's terrifying tale of a hypnotist (almost a mad scientist) bidding a somnambulist (almost a man-made creature) to kill certain people in a small town brought the other vital element to science fiction film: visual style. *The Cabinet of Dr. Caligari* (1919), held by some as the first horror film, made revolutionary use of cubist expressionism, skewed perspective, and bizarre visuals that paled even the most whimsical of previous fantastic films.

Using creepy streets, nightmarish shadows, and a truly terrifying monster, Weine and his crew from Germany's UFA Studios made a movie that, although it was ridiculed by the stodgy film establishment, would influence a surreal universe of frightening flicks to come. Caligari's scriptwriter, a young Fritz Lang, learned his visual lessons well. In eight years, using the same crew and a cinematographer, he would create the first true milestone of science fiction cinema—a terrifying vision of a futuristic metropolis.

The crew of Captain Nemo's Nautilus *surveys the scenery in this superb silent version of* 20,000 Leagues Under the Sea *(1916).*

VIVA LA DYSTOPIA

In October 1924, filmmaker Fritz Lang was cooling his heels aboard the deck of the SS *Deutschland* from Berlin, waiting to dock in New York Harbor. The war had ended six years before and still German ships had to sail through an ocean of red tape before disembarking. Lang didn't mind, however. The night view of the (even then) fabled New York skyline was dazzlingly futuristic to a European. But this European had already been thinking about the future as his fatherland reeled out of the rubble of postwar reparations. He had recently finished reading the book *Wir* by the Russian writer Yevgeny Zamyatin about a society run by a coldhearted machine, the ultimate in scientific reason. Czech playwright Karel Capek had introduced the word "Robotnic" (forced laborer)

> **"I enjoyed it beyond my wildest dreams."**
>
> **—Sir Arthur Conan Doyle (creator of Sherlock Holmes and author of the science fiction classic *The Lost World*) on Fritz Lang's *Metropolis* (1926)**

into the European theaters with his play *R.U.R.* (for Rossum's Universal Robots).

These deckside musings (and a subsequent visit to New York's Times Square) led Lang to a collaboration with his wife, science fiction writer Thea Von Harbou, on a tale of pessimistic prophecy whose very raison d'être would be expressionism (the antithesis of all things mechanized), whose plot would be a melodrama of class struggle, and whose visuals would be like nothing anyone had ever witnessed.

Lang's film of the year 2026, *Metropolis*, runs like a living machine. The city's surface is a glittering marvel. Painstakingly crafted miniatures created the illusion of suspended superhighways threading through canyons of impossibly tall skyscrapers, so

With a name like Rotwang, you've got to be a mad scientist. Rudolf Klein-Rogge admires his own demented handiwork before the last stages of soul and skin combine in Metropolis (1926).

high that planes pass under speeding cars on connecting bridges. (A car ride through this scene was accomplished by massive amounts of scenery dragged past the car windows.) Steam whistles blow in clusters as big as organ pipes, neon lights dazzle in every configuration, and the very architecture seems to spread endlessly out and vault endlessly up.

Overlooking it all, in a sumptuously furnished, basketball court–size, art deco office that would impress Mike Ovitz, is the master of Metropolis, the industrialist Jon Frederson (a reptilian-looking Alfred Abel). While the master coolie controls the techno-paradise below (witness film's first use of rear-screen projection as Frederson chats with a foreman on his videophone), his naive son Freder (Gustav Fröelich) idles away his time in pleasure gardens surrounded by lascivious beauties and running races in a stadium (a scene cut from the American print that required a colossal 37,633 extras). But far beneath the city's surface lies the burning heart of Metropolis, its subcity of zombielike workers and the hideous machinery that enslaves them. When a beautiful nurse named Maria (Brigitte Helm) brings a flock of miserable workers' children to the surface and confronts Freder, the innocent scion follows her back down into the catacombs of hell.

Hell is where Lang's crew went to town. Even more amazing than their miniature magic worked above is this sunless, multi-level sprawl of soulless barracks; house-size elevators; giant, steam-belching machines; and a towering, control-covered furnace that changes into a gaping mouth of the murderous god Molloch. Here, the "kniffe" (photographic trickery) used by special effects pioneer Eugene Shufftan (who, like Lang, had studied architecture and illustration) employed a two-lens camera to capture live actors with mirror reflections of models or painted backdrops to incredible effect. To create the effect of a technical malfunction that fries all the workers on watch with electricity, Shufftan placed a high-frequency spark machine mere inches from the camera lens and made arcs of sparks seem to dance across every inch of the structure.

Later, in the workers' plaza, in front of a gong ten feet (3m) in diameter, Freder watches Maria preach to the downtrodden masses on the biblical Tower of Babel. For the accompanying biblical flashback Lang needed six thousand head-shaved extras. When only one thousand unemployed men offered their services, cameramen Karl Freund (who would one day direct Boris Karloff in *The Mummy*, 1932) and Gunther Rittau expressionistically refracted the footage of them six times. Freder, like the audience on- and off-screen, is mesmerized by the sermon.

None of us knows the half of it. In a hulking, windowless, gingerbread-style house (with a huge Satanic hex-sign painted on it), out of place against the faceless industrial wasteland, lives Rotwang (Rudolf Klein-Rogge), a demented scientist with wild white hair and one deformed, rubber-gloved hand (something Peter Sellers would take inspiration from in *Dr. Strangelove*, 1964). In scenes that were cut from the original release, it was revealed that Rotwang was an embittered rival for the affections of Freder's mother, Hel (Paramount Studios was afraid that stateside audi-

ences would snicker at her name). What remains intact is Rotwang's insidious plot with Jon Frederson to transform an incredibly sensuous yet sinister-looking, high-breasted female robot into a flesh-covered impostor of Maria who will stir the workers to revolt so that the surface powers will have an excuse to impose martial law below.

Art directors Otto Hunte, Erich Kettlehut, and Karl Volbrecht's lab for Rotwang truly rivals Dr. Frankenstein's pad. In one of sci-fi's greatest moments, the kidnapped Maria, strapped under rings of metal and hooked up with electrodes, lends her brain waves to the transforming robot through concentric rings of electricity that scrawl up and down the cyborg as flesh adheres to its metal skeleton. Here, Shufftan used glass tubes rigged on pulleys and filled with electrified gas to create an effect that will literally burn its way into your memory.

What happens? Let's just say that the robot Maria does a dance so lewd (in pasties no less) that the overwrought workers tear apart their machinery, wreaking chaos and a horribly realistic flood (literally ripping up the concrete floor) upon their children on the dwelling level below. As statues of the Seven Deadly Sins wrench themselves into life off the pedestals of a cathedral above...well, that would be telling.

Let it suffice to say that this is not a movie to miss. After a 310-day shoot and a $5 million budget, Lang had created a parable so powerful that Hitler himself became Lang's biggest fan. Luckily, when Joseph Goebbels offered the director control of the budding Nazi film industry, the master of *Metropolis*, knowing a real future nightmare when he saw one, fled to Hollywood via la belle France.

THE GOLDEN AGE BEGINS

Before sci-fi émigrés like Lang, Freund, and Veidt ever hunkered down to their first hamburger (aside from Hamburg), another German made a home in America for the very best in science fiction and horror. By 1912, entrepreneur Carl Laemmle had established Universal Studios, and under his paternal eye, dozens of European film émigrés were welcomed to Hollywood's waiting, mercenary arms. Such classically frightening films as *The Hunchback of Notre Dame* (1923), *The Phantom of the Opera* (1925), *London After Midnight* (1927), and *Dracula* (1931) made Universal Horror a household name.

Following on *Dracula's* capetails, Uncle Carl (as he was affectionately called) next sent Universal into the laboratory to see what it could make of yet another literary classic, Mary Wollstonecraft Shelley's *Frankenstein*, this time riding the line between science fiction and horror. James Whale was at the directorial helm and Colin Clive played the high-strung chemical galvanist Dr. Henry Frankenstein. The creature was originally to be played by long-time stage actor and bit player (as well as the son of an English diplomat) William Henry Pratt.

The great Boris Karloff, as we know him, took the role of the monster when Whale, intrigued by Karloff's bone structure, approached him in the Universal commissary. The wordless part (unlike its chatty literary predecessor), the reason why Bela Lugosi had rejected the role, paid a mere $125 a week, but it was a steady gig. Hermann Rosse's superb gothic sets, John P. Fulton and Ken Strickfaden's special effects sparking through art director Charles D. Hall's take on Frankenstein's bizarre laboratory, Arthur Edeson's delight-fully dreary black-and-white cinematography, and Dwight Frye's portrayal of the murderously childlike hunchback, Fritz, all made it memorable. Karloff made it unforget-table, working wonders as the creature created from criminals' corpses and a murderer's brain, and brought to life by electricity. Nor was Karloff likely to forget the pain of creation.

Makeup wizard (and ex–professional baseball player) Jack Pierce created a completely believable look for this man-made man. The creature's skull had been crudely cut off at the top (Henry was no surgeon by trade), allowing the mistakenly abnormal brain to be inserted. Two giant staples seemed to close the handiwork. Postmortem research led Pierce to the detail that blood distended the arms and legs of a

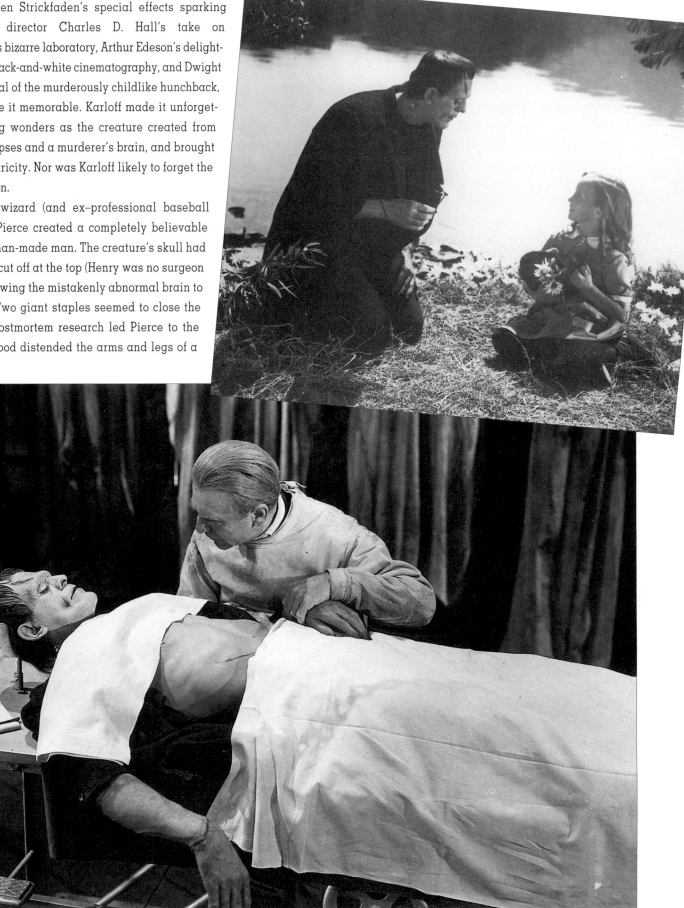

TOP: Little girls don't float quite as easily as flowers do. What starts as a tender encounter doesn't end that way in Frankenstein (1931). BOTTOM: Edward Van Sloan examines makeup man Jack Pierce's handiwork (aka Boris Karloff).

THE THING THAT WOULDN'T DIE, OR, FRANKENLINE

1910: Clownish, neckless, in pale makeup, and boasting a head of crazy silver hair, Charles Ogle was the first to do the monster mash as a creature "created in a caldron of blazing chemicals" who considerately dies in the end so that his maker can get on with his honeymoon in Thomas Alva Edison's film company's production of Frankenstein.

1936: Al Ritz of the Ritz Brothers plays Frank on ice in figure skater Sonja Henie's film debut, One in a Million.

1939: Boris Karloff makes his last appearance as the monster. In Son of Frankenstein, Henry's son Wolf (Basil Rathbone) raises the dead with the help of demented, deformed shepherd Ygor (Bela Lugosi).

1942: Henry's second son, Ludwig (Cedric Hardwicke), takes over the family pursuit when The Ghost of Frankenstein demands a new brain for his creation (Lon Chaney, Jr.).

1942: A reconstructed cat kidnaps a baby bird and it's up to Mighty Mouse to save the day in the animated short Frankenstein's Cat.

1957: Christopher Lee's portrayal of the creature and Peter Cushing's mad doc hit the nail on the head thanks to this gorgeously colored, Hammer Films production of The Curse of Frankenstein.

1957: When a mad scientist reanimates the body of a hot-rodder killed in a car wreck, he promises to take his creation to lover's lane to pick out a handsome, new head in I Was a Teenage Frankenstein.

1960: What nearsighted bumbler would stumble on a baron's castle where a mad scientist has plans to upgrade his brain from a chicken brain in his current creation? Mr. Magoo in Magoo Meets Frankenstein.

1960: From Mexico comes the story of an evil ex-convict who breaks the good doctor out of prison to help him wreak havoc on his enemies via a resuscitated monster with a melted face in Orlak—The Hands of Frankenstein.

1961: Woody Woodpecker battles a mechanical chicken-plucker with a strange resemblance to you-know-who in Franken-Stymied.

Marty Feldman, Peter Boyle, and Gene Wilder (left to right) prepare to do a little "Puttin' on the Ritz" in *Young Frankenstein*.

1973: Michael Sarrazin portrays the handsome and articulate creature that Shelley brought to life in prose, with an all-star cast that includes Ralph Richardson, John Gielgud, James Mason, Agnes Moorehead, and Jane Seymour in Frankenstein: The True Story.

1974: An asylum setting provides the good doctor with body parts, but his creation (Dave Prowse) ends up dismembered by the incensed inmates in Frankenstein and the Monster from Hell.

1974: Only from Mel Brooks could come a creation as comic as this. Gene Wilder is the perfect hysteria-prone genius and Peter Boyle is perhaps the only creature who ever sang "Puttin' on the Ritz" in the delightful Young Frankenstein.

1974: Only from Andy Warhol could come a tale as twisted as the doc who thrills in violat-ing female corpses and wants to start a super-race but makes a monster with the head of a farm boy who wants to be a monk in Flesh for Frankenstein.

Of all the icons that science fiction and horror have created, none has been as enduring or as exploited as that tall, strong, silent type we've come to know, love, and fear. Let's look at just some of Mary's monster's movie descendants.

1943: This time it's Bela's turn to wear the heavy boots while Lon Chaney, Jr., plays tortured Lawrence Talbot, the Wolf Man, seeking the secret of "true death" in Frankenstein Meets the Wolf Man.

1944: Boris is back and badder than ever as an escaped lunatic, Dr. Neimann, who avenges himself on his enemies with the help of Dracula (John Carradine), the Wolf Man (Lon Chaney, Jr.), and the Frankenstein Monster (Glenn Strange) in House of Frankenstein

1948: In one of their funniest films, Abbott and Costello Meet Frankenstein, the duo tangles with the terror trio (Lugosi, Chaney, and Strange) when a sinister doctor needs a weaker and more pliable brain for his creature....Oh, Lou!!!

1964: From Japan comes a weird one. The atomic bomb dropped on Hiroshima revives the creature's heart, which is mistakenly ingested by a young boy twenty years later. He grows to monstrous size, eats cattle, tosses tanks, and fights a giant reptile let loose by an earthquake in Furankenshutain Tai Baragon.

1966: Maria Frankenstein flees to the Wild West after her father's experiments , only to continue his work. She puts an artificial brain in a muscle-bound member of a notorious outlaw gang in Jesse James Meets Frankenstein's Daughter.

Gunslingers are no match for Frankenmuscle in the crossover *Jesse James Meets Frankenstein's Daughter* (1966).

1967: Dr. Frankenstein (Peter Cushing) takes a heartbroken, crippled girl (Playboy playmate Susan Denberg) and gives her the brain of her guillotined boyfriend. The result is a babe who seduces men only to hack them up with a meat cleaver in Frankenstein Created Woman.

1971: Creation Italian style. Home from medical school, Tanya Frankenstein creates a creature to satisfy her sexual yearnings in La Figlia Di Frankenstein (Daughter of Frankenstein).

1972: Dr. Stein takes his lab assistant's quadriplegic, Vietnam-vet boyfriend and turns him into a disemboweling creature who is eventually ripped apart by Dobermans in Blackenstein.

1983: Yes, Zsa-Zsa Gabor and Aldo Ray support as Dr. F. (Donald Pleasence) finds himself evicted from the manor due to back taxes in Frankenstein's Great Aunt Tillie.

1984: Ah, at last a deft and literary adaptation with Robert Powel as the doc and David Warner as the creature in Frankenstein.

1984: This loving James Whale tribute from Tim Burton boasts a boy who brings his faithful dog Sparky back from the dead. Things don't get much creepier or cuter than Frankenweenie.

1990: It had to happen eventually. When his girlfriend dies this doc tries out her head on the bodies of various ladies of the night in Frankenhooker.

1993: The last good adaptation stars a sympathetic Randy Quaid as a creature who needs some understanding from his arrogant creator, played by master of handsome maniacs Patrick Bergin, in Frankenstein.

1994: Though Kenneth Branaugh's passionate Victor, discards his shirt in many a scene, Robert De Niro's grim creature doesn't quite discard his New York accent in Mary Shelley's Frankenstein.

criminal buried alive. Sleeves and trousers were shortened and fingernails painted black. Those famous metal electrode inputs were inserted on either side of the creature's neck (the makeup application left Karloff with scars for the rest of his life).

Karloff endured more. Hot paraffin covered his eyelids to give them a reptilian look. A big box of a skull and a bulbous brow were cemented to his forehead. Layer upon layer of cotton soaked in collodion, putty, and greenish greasepaint (which appeared gray on black-and-white film) entombed his face and neck. Hidden wire clamps pulled his mouth out and down. Plaster covered his hands and arms. His lean frame was padded to the max. To give him the lumbering walk, steel struts stiffened his legs and a pair of eleven-and-a-half-pound (5kg) asphalt spreader's boots weighted his feet.

Karloff sweated away twenty pounds (9kg) during shooting, perhaps because he had to lug around an extra eighteen inches (46cm) of height and sixty-two pounds (28kg) of heft for the role. For the scene where the creature carries his maker up to the mill, soon to be swarmed by villagers, Whale insisted that the already burdened Karloff haul the real Clive, take after take. By the end of filming, Karloff was in the hospital for a spinal fusion. Producers deemed his mute part so insignificant that he wasn't even invited to the film's premiere. But the crowds knew better. Pierce's legendary makeup and Karloff's childlike emoting and animal rage made the creature the star of the show. A sequel was a cinch. Thus, the film's original happy ending of Dr. Frankenstein's father toasting his son's health was replaced with a scene where monster and master seem to die in a burning mill.

It's rare that a sequel is better than the original, but *Bride of Frankenstein* (1935) is both scarier and funnier than its predecessor. Creature and creator survived a fire and a fall—the creature by virtue of the flooded basement and Henry by virtue of dumb luck. Henry is seduced by the eccentric Dr. Praetorious, who has been doing his own experiments growing tiny people, into joining forces to create a...a...a...WOMAN! Though the role was originally offered to the celebrated mad scientist from *The Invisible Man* (1933), Claude Rains, it went to Ernest Thesiger when Rains turned it down. The scowling Thesiger, who reportedly spent off-screen time sitting in a corner doing his needlepoint, rides the onscreen line between camp and truly creepy like an expert surfer, stealing nearly every scene he's in.

This time Boris bagged $2,500 a week and, despite his fierce objections, spoke. As he later said, "My argument was that if the Monster had any impact or charm it was because he was inarticulate—this great, lumbering, inarticulate creature." When a fleeing creature takes refuge with a lonely, old, blind hermit, so begins a vocal education and some of the tenderest scenes a monster ever made. Later, when encountering (and drinking wine with) Dr. Praetorious while the doctor is grave-robbing in a crypt (the same cavernous arched set used for *Dracula*'s 1931 roost), the creature even quips a heartfelt pearl of wisdom in response to the unfazed doctor's plan to make a woman from the dead: "Made from dead. I love dead, hate living." Originally, the quirky doc did him one better, speaking of his own love for the dead, but censors thought it looked a little too necrophilic, so out it went.

Fortunately the appearance of the blushing bride was left in the movie. Whale had originally wanted *Metropolis'* Brigitte Helm

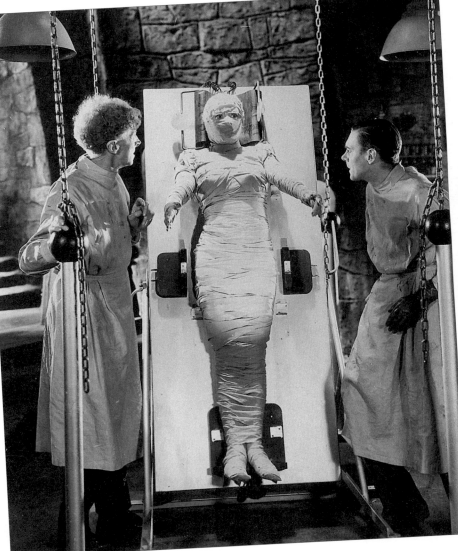

OPPOSITE: *The face that launched a thousand shrieks, Boris Karloff looking demonically undead in* Frankenstein *(1931)*. ABOVE: *The poster proclaimed, "Warning! The Monster demands a Mate!" Dr. Praetorious (Ernest Thesiger, left) and Dr. Henry Frankenstein (Colin Clive, right) try to deliver a wrapped Elsa Lanchester in* Bride of Frankenstein *(1935)*.

or thinking man's sex symbol Louise Brooks for the role. When they were unavailable, Whale brought in his friend, actress Elsa Lanchester, whose husband, Charles Laughton, had cut quite a figure himself as the insane vivisector in *Island of Lost Souls* (1933).

While Lanchester modeled her birdlike movements on Helm's evil Maria from *Metropolis* and a hissing swan who was the bully of a lake that Lanchester frequented in London's Regent Park, Jack Pierce looked to ancient Egypt's Queen Nefertiti for the look of the female creation. As Lanchester remembered, "The monster make-up took three hours for my face alone. My hair was stiffened into a topsy-like mop and was made to stick out backward on a little cage. I was then bound in yards and yards of bandage, all carefully done by a nurse. This took one hour. I used to get very tired in this curious form of costume, because it was difficult to move and impossible to sit down or walk." For three days of shooting Lanchester suffered, having to be fed by her dresser and hold her bladder all day. Her stand-in didn't face the claustrophobia quite as well, at one point screaming hysterically until all the bandages were removed.

Karloff had his own cross to bear. The forty-eight-year-old arthritic actor dislocated his hip when a protective rubber suit he wore for the opening scene semi-inflated and made him fall. Pierce burned off some of the creature's hair, revealing nine more clamps along his singed skull. This time close-ups showed huge pores in the creature's skin because Pierce layered cheesecloth under Karloff's makeup. For thirty-two straight shooting days, Karloff's glamorous schedule went something like this:

4:30 A.M.—Karloff awakes, indulges in cold shower, infrared treatments for left hip, and black coffee.

5:20 A.M.—Star leaves for studio.

6:00 A.M.—Cosmetician preps Karloff's face so that makeup won't leave him a real monster.

7:00 A.M.—Dr. Pierce-enstein makes his five-hour magic.

12:30 P.M.—Karloff entombed into boots, fitted into leg struts, and strapped into body pads.

1:30 P.M.—It's tea and sandwich break.

2:00 P.M.—With pores painted over, wearing sixty-two pounds (28kg) of makeup and costume, under blistering hot lights, Karloff begins work.

7:00 P.M.—Filming stops. Makeup comes off with oil and acetic acid.

8:00 P.M.—Once home, Karloff indulges in cold shower, more tea, more infrared treatment, and massage for circulation in legs and pain in hip.

9:30 P.M.—Star in bed looking over script for next day's shoot.

His pain and patience paid off. With its wonderful acting, tongue-in-cheek dialogue, sumptuous sets, electrifying lab scene (this time with a kite bringing the lightning to the monster), and the first full orchestral score for a sci-fi film (by Franz Waxman), *Bride of Frankenstein* is practically perfect. Only its fiery ending remains flawed to the keenest eye. It seems that original footage had the monster killing Henry, Henry's fiancée, Dr. Praetorious, the female creation, and himself in a laboratory explosion. But a sequel needs a sequel. And Henry and his betrothed were allowed to live...though if you look closely at the tumbling rubble you can still see Colin Clive being buried by it.

A IS FOR ATOMIC

Like Camelot before it, the golden age of horror and science fiction didn't last forever. Mad scientists and monsters movies adapted from the literary wellspring, such as *Dr. Jekyll and Mr. Hyde* (1932), *The Invisible Man*, and *Island of Lost Souls*, gradually crawled back to their librar-atories (though they always came out for remakes). For more than a decade the experimental amalgams of horror and science fiction continued, though since they were concocted by Hollywood mercenaries rather than science fiction visionaries, the results gradually became rusty.

Then on August 6, 1945, Hiroshima's atomic death knell gave the dangers of science a whole new meaning for the world. Governments raced each other to harness the practical powers of the split atom now that its savagery had been unleashed on a civilian population. Sold as a futuristic tool, most accepted it as that. But others were uneasy. Warner Bros. producer Ted Sherdeman had been a staff officer to General Douglas MacArthur during World War II and remembered that when he received the news of the 100,000 persons slaughtered at Hiroshima and Nagasaki, "I just went over to the curb and started to throw up."

> *"When man entered the Atomic Age he opened the door into a new world. What he may eventually find, no one can predict."*
>
> —Edmund Gwenn as Dr. Medford in *Them!* (1954)

After the war, Sherdeman was hungry to do a film that would bring up the possibilities of atomic radiation's darker side. When George Worthing Yates' story of an army of giant, radiation-mutated ants invading New York and hiding out in the subway system circulated through Warner Bros., he bit. "The idea appealed to me very much because, aside from man, ants are the only creatures in the world who plan and wage war," he recalled. Little did he know that making the film would be a battle all its own.

Yates was paid $2,500 a week for ten weeks to come in and make a movie from his book. Halfway through, however, it became apparent that Yates was a bit too heady with cinematic possibilities. "It had some ants in it," confessed the producer, "but it was one of those things that would have cost $42 million to produce." Five more weeks were wasted as studio head Jack Warner insisted on getting his money's worth from the floundering writer.

Sherdeman next brought in Russell Hughes to adapt the failed script. Out went New York. In came New Mexico's Jornada del Muerto Desert, northwest of the Trinity site at Almagordo, nine years after the first atomic test on July 16, 1945. Hughes was off to a great start, beginning the story almost as a film noir mystery with a highway patrol helicopter discovering the lone figure of a catatonic, six-year-old girl clutching her doll as she stumbled through the desert wastes. Then, twenty pages into his work, Hughes died at home in front of his television.

Sherdeman took over writing the story. The hard-boiled cops find the girl's parents' trailer smashed and bloodied with no money taken but sugar cubes scattered and strange footprints in the sand.

Then they hear unearthly, high-pitched howls on the desolate and dusty desert winds. They discover that a nearby general store was ripped apart, seemingly for sugar, with the proprietor's shotgun barrels twisted like spaghetti and the man himself with his "neck and back broken, skull fractured, chest crushed, with enough formic acid in him to kill twenty men." They bring in not only the FBI but a father-and-daughter duo of myrmecologists (ant entomologists to laymen) to examine the footprint casting, horrified at the implications of what they think might be happening. The suspense mounts until the twelve-foot (3.5m) long ants make their appearance.

A story this juicy called for not only a color release but the now-popular (since *Bwana Devil* had started the craze two years earlier) 3-D treatment. Sherdeman's enthusiasm was less than matched when, on a Warner Bros.' lot sidewalk, Jack Warner's assistant, Steve Trilling, pointed to a swarm of ants and demanded, "You mean, you wanna make a movie about these things?" When Sherdeman assented, Trilling sighed, "For Christ's sake!" and stalked away.

To win the support of Trilling and his boss, Sherdeman went to two young entomologists at nearby UCLA and enlisted their support in creating a short documentary film that showed ants' awesome strength (lifting twenty times their own weight), aggression (fighting another ant to the death for days at a time), and military behavior (accomplishing tasks with incredible organization). In Sherdeman's script Professor Medford (wonderfully played by Edmund Gwenn) shows such a film to an astonished audience of military and political leaders to make them see how serious the situation is. When Sherdeman did the same with Warner, the mogul walked out after two minutes, muttering "Hell, who needs this?"

Now desperate, Sherdeman went to Larry Meiggs at the Warner Bros. art department with photographs of harvester ants. The resulting three-foot (91.5cm) long model with movable mandible, head, and antennae (placed in a surprise box on Trilling's desk) got such a good response that a screen test was immediately shot. But when Warner saw the celluloid, he put the film (and the ant) up for sale.

Things got worse. When Twentieth Century Fox wanted to buy the rights to the movie, Warner Bros. honcho Walter McCuhan did something novel: he took the script home to read—and liked it. He canceled the sale and brought in Gordon Douglas, veteran comedy director of *Our Gang* and *Laurel and Hardy*, to lens it. Douglas told Sherdeman that he thought the creepy script would be a perfect vehicle for Martin and Lewis. Sherdeman "went out and got awfully drunk, and then I started casting."

Sherdeman's last act as producer was to cast Gwenn as the scientist and spokesman for sanity. But Gwenn was best known as Santa Claus in *Miracle on 34th Street* (1947), and when Sherdeman hung tough against Warner's assertion that the actor was too old, the writer/producer was demoted to just writer. Luckily, Douglas worked closely with the former producer, changing the location of the film's ending (as the entire U.S. military chases a flying queen ant to Los Angeles) from the amusement park at Santa Monica Pier to the cheaper and much eerier maze of ducts in the city's drainage system.

James Whitmore, as the tough cop with a tender spot for kids, and James Arness, who had already followed Karloff's footsteps as the monster in *The Thing (from Another World)* (1951), as the FBI agent with the hots for the daughter scientist (Joan Weldon), were inspired casting for this fast-paced, near-documentary-style sci-fi thriller. If you look closely, you can spot Leonard Nimoy as a teletype machine operator and Fess Parker as a jet pilot being held for psychiatric observation after seeing the flying ants. Olin Howlin, who plays a drying-out drunk who sees the ants in the spillway outside his hospital window, provides comic relief.

Douglas believed that "if you don't give an audience something to laugh at once in a while, they're going to find something, maybe the wrong thing."

Them! doesn't offer much else to laugh about. Bronislaw Kaper's jangling soundtrack and the creatures' eerie wails (layered audio tracks of bird sounds) do their disquieting job. Visually, the giant ants do theirs, looking especially ghastly when crushing humans in their mandibles. Special effects designer Ralph Ayers built two behemoth, lever-controlled ants: a whole one for long shots, the other a front portion mounted on a boom for close-ups. "You would have a shot where the ant comes into the picture," said Douglas, "and if you glanced behind the creature you would see about twenty guys all sweating like hell."

Colored a purple shade of green, the ants were made even more lifelike by the bubbling blue-and-red mixture of soapy liquid coursing through their eyes. It was a lot of trouble to go through, especially when the Warner Bros. brass told Douglas and his crew to scale back to black-and-white film only two days before shooting began in the Mojave Desert. Luckily, the absence of color just makes the movie seem more like a documentary. Douglas had asked his editor Thomas Reilly if the ants looked honest. "As honest as twelve-foot [3.5m] ants can look," Reilly replied.

IRREVERENCE FOR THINGS PAST

After Universal's golden age had tarnished but before nuclear mutants and invading aliens had come on the scene, there was one staple that fed millions of red-blooded American sci-fi viewers—and it sounded like what most of them were given for breakfast by their mommies each morning. The science fiction serial was a twenty-minute installment of riveting, comic-book action and bargain-basement special effects sandwiched between the cartoon, comedy short, coming attractions, and B picture at the local Saturday matinee. Sci-fi serials had a long life, from as early as 1915 in The Exploits of Elaine *(where Pearl White battled the Clutching Hand and its lethal death ray)* to The Zombies of the Stratosphere *(1952) (where you can also spot Leonard Nimoy). Those titles just about tell it all.* With twelve to fifteen weekly installments during a hot summer, serials would give a kid cool futuristic technology, nail-biting cliffhangers, and good and bad guys aplenty.

Villains with sinister names like Ming the Merciless, Professor Strang, the Crimson Ghost, Zolok, Killer Kane, Unga Kahn, the Scorpion, Boroff, Jason Grood, Mephisto, Vic Murkland, the Spider Lady, Professor Zorn, Sir Eric Hazarious, and Dr. Satan hailed from such sinister climes as Morovania, the sewers of Paris, the House of Mystery, the heights of Magnetic Mountain, the depths of Atlantis, the planet Mongo, and of course Japan and Nazi Germany. Fighting for truth, justice, and the American way were

PATHÉ

THE MYSTERIOUS SUPER-CRIMINAL IN
THE EXPLOITS OF ELAINE
is arousing a perfect fever of interest. Who is he? When and how will he be caught? These are questions everyone is asking. The greatest detective stories in America are now made into the greatest motion picture serial ever produced. The result is an amazing success.

BOOK ELAINE NOW AND SAVE YOURSELF FUTURE REGRETS.

THE PATHÉ EXCHANGE, Inc.,
(FORMERLY THE ECLECTIC FILM CO.)
110 WEST 40th. ST.   NEW YORK.

Who is this mad genius and what the heck is that gadget? Only the Saturday matinee viewers of early sci-fi serials knew the answers.

actors as diverse as John Wayne, Alan Ladd, singing cowboy Gene Autry, and Olympic gold-medalist swimmer Buster Crabbe. They portrayed heroes such as Buck Rogers, Captain America, Dick Tracy, Tarzan, the Green Hornet, Spy Smasher, Batman, G-Man, Superman, the Phantom, Flash Gordon, and King of the Texas Rangers. These icons of the preadolescent set surmounted incredible techno-obstacles week after week. One serial's scientist hero might realize that a planet's Clay People speak a backward version of the tongue of the lost tribes of the Gobi Desert. Another might swoop along with a futuristic jet pack or beam up in a way much different than Captain Kirk ever did. While one hero battled the hawk-men in their floating Sky City, at a matinee across town another serial savior might take on an army of zombified slaves. Meteors on a collision course with Earth were averted at the last second. Insidious plots to take over the world with nerve gas, an invisibility belt, killer robots, death rays, and a reanimation formula were thankfully thwarted at the last possible moment. And if the costumes looked a little cheesy or the spaceships wobbled on the wires they hung from, viewers were willing to suspend their disbelief, too.

With the advent of the boob tube (a futuristic weapon to bring Earth to its knees by robbing the human race of their intelligence), serials went the way of classic mad scientists, marauding Martians, and myrmecological mutants. Well, not for everybody.

After *Them!* had its premiere, Warner assembled his attending producers and directors and said, "Anybody who wants to make more ant pictures will go to Republic [a small studio known for B-movies]." But the ant picture not only grossed more moola than any other movie out of Warner Bros. that year, it spawned a whole subgenre of radiation mutations through the rest of the decade.

Tarantula (1955) came crawling after, eating cattle as it came. *The Deadly Mantis* (1957) flew in to New York City from the North Pole to wreak some havoc. Future horror/sci-fi master Roger Corman added crustaceans that had the ability to speak in the voice of anyone whose head they had recently ingested in *Attack of the Crab Monsters* (1957). Giant wasps packed a wallop in *Monster from Green Hell* (1957). Giant scorpions invaded Mexico City in *The Black Scorpion* (1957). Giant grasshoppers (fed on vegetables contaminated with radioactive isotopes) chowed down on Chicago in *The Beginning of the End* (1957). And in Japan, where they had experienced the nuclear nightmare firsthand, irradiated monsters ruled for even longer. Inoshiro Honda's *Godzilla, King of the Monsters* (1956) started a successful sixteen-film career (thanks also to actor Huro Nakajima in a one-hundred-pound [45kg] costume) of taking on Tokyo and other giant mutants. Before he was through he had bested the likes of the giant pterodactyl *Rodan* (1957), giant moth *Mothra* (1962), giant turtle *Gammera, The Invincible* (1966), and giant shrimp *Megalon* (1976), and had become a Japanese screen star second only to Toshiro Mifune.

And for the studio execs who laughed at giant ants as villains, *Phase IV* (1974) raked in the bucks showing hyperintelligent, normal-size ants in the Arizona desert battling, beating, and transforming the scientists who discover them. You'd have to have an ant brain to doubt the power of science fiction.

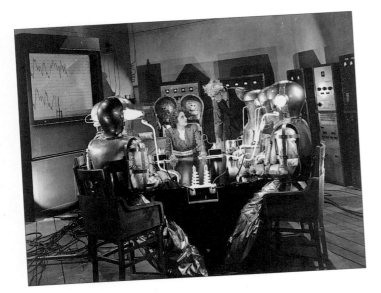

ABOVE: Son of Serial: A distinctly demented looking Boris Karloff would like to help Amanda Duff communicate with the dead in The Devil Commands (1941).

DAYS OF FUTURE PAST

A long time ago (well, only 1944) in a galaxy far away (actually, Modesto, California), George Lucas was born. His dad, a stationery store owner, bought a TV in 1954 and young George was soon hooked on reruns of old science fiction serials. Little did the kid who was watching Flash and Buck battle for a better galaxy suspect that he would be using those memories to make one of the most successful science fiction movies ever made (after a galaxy of changes to his original idea). In high school he was a race car buff until a near-fatal crash (his small Fiat was hit broadside by a Chevy Impala) reminded him how short life was.

Lucas' days at Modesto Junior College led to his admission to USC's film school, where

> "Star Wars, which opened yesterday...is the most beautiful movie serial ever made. It is both an apotheosis of Flash Gordon serials and a witty critique that makes associations with a variety of literature."
>
> —Movie critic Vincent Canby from his *New York Times* review of *Star Wars* (1977)

he made an award-winning student film about a totalitarian futuristic society called *THX1138:4EB (The Electronic Labyrinth)*. Interning at Warner Bros., he came under the guidance of filmmaker Francis Ford Coppola and made a documentary on the making of Coppola's *The Rain People* (1969). He then borrowed one of its stars, Robert Duvall, for a Warner Bros.–funded remake of his moody college film, which became a cult favorite. Cowriting and directing *American Graffiti* (1973) for Universal Pictures (which cost $700,000 and raked in $145 million) made Lucas bankable. And when negotiations turned problematic in working with his old mentor on *Apocalypse Now* (1979), George's thoughts went back to those serials he used to sit watching.

At first, Lucas claims, he "wanted to make a Flash Gordon movie with all the trimmings, but I couldn't obtain the rights to the character. So I began researching and went back and found where Alex Raymond [creator of the Flash Gordon comics] had got his idea from." Reading Edgar Rice Burroughs' *John Carter on Mars*, Lucas went further and perused a 1905 book that inspired Burroughs called *Gulliver on Mars* by Edwin Arnold.

Afternoons in 1972 were spent researching these books as well as myths, fairy tales, heroic exploits, and social psychology, while mornings gave Lucas time to write. By May 1973, Lucas had a thirteen-page plot summary set in the twenty-third century about the elderly combat generals Luke Skywalker and Annakin Starkiller, the sole survivors of the Jedi Knights' destruction by the Evil Empire, who join forces with Princess Leia Aguiae to train teens as the new Jedi warriors. Universal passed on Lucas' $25,000 screenplay, but Alan Ladd, Jr., at Twentieth Century Fox offered him $50,000 to write, $100,000 to direct, and a budget of $8.5 million. By

ABOVE: *They were lovable (and merchandizable) alright, but boy were those droids uncomfortable to fit into! Anthony Daniels (C3PO) and Kenny Baker (R2D2) deserved Oscars for endurance in* Star Wars *(1977). RIGHT: Chewbacca (Peter Mayhew), Princess Leia (Carrie Fisher), and Han Solo (Harrison Ford) brace themselves for the Millennium Falcon's jump into hyperspace.*

May 1974, a screenplay was ready, entitled *Adventures of the Starkiller: Episode One of the Star Wars*. Eighteen-year-old Annakin Starkiller and his older brother, Biggs, would set off to rescue their father, Kane, from the Emperor (modeled on Richard Nixon), while eleven-year-old Princess Leia took up most of the storyline and Han Solo was nothing but a green, gilled, noseless monster. By January 1975, Lucas had whittled down his script to focus on Luke (now melded with traits of the former Annakin character) and Solo (now a Correlian pirate), who had a strange resemblance on paper to Francis Ford Coppola. By August of that year, the evil general Darth Vader and the kindly former Jedi, Obi-Wan Kenobi, had been split from one character. By early 1976, Biggs' function of fellow pilot and brotherly rivalry went to the dashing Han Solo.

The final plot (for those who have been living in a cave for the past two decades) follows a boy named Luke Skywalker who yearns to leave his uncle's desert ranch in a distant galaxy that is both futuristic and familiarly American. Fate intervenes when two fugitive androids pursued by soldiers of the Evil Empire cross his path. One of them is programmed with a secret plea for help from a six-teen-year-old captive rebel princess named Leia to Obi-Wan Kenobi, a Jedi Knight warrior from past battles with the Empire. The mysterious old man, whom Luke knows as Ben Kenobi the hermit, saves Luke's life after the boy had gone out looking for one of the droids who had wandered off.

After Luke's home and family are destroyed he and Ben decide to go to Leia's aid and enlist the support of a cynical, self-involved mercenary named Han Solo and his tall, lycanthropic copilot, Chewbacca (a Wookie—a cross between a cat, dog, and gorilla from a damp jungle planet where they inhabit inflatable houses in giant trees), and his spaceship, the *Millennium Falcon*. Together, these good guys (with Leia rescued from the clutches of the Dark Side) will face impossible odds against the Evil Empire's insidious political leader— a hulking, shrouded, helmeted, heavy-breathing, masked commander named Darth Vader—and all his storm troopers. In their battle to destroy the Empire's Death Star, a behemoth space station with the power to obliterate an entire planet, all will be transformed (especially young Luke) by the unifying power of all life, a.k.a. the Force. The rest is film history.

To weave his tale, Lucas' mind and pen (he always wrote on blue-and-green lined paper in longhand) gave new meaning to the word *eclectic*. He borrowed from everything, everyone, and everywhere to fill his futuristic universe. When the sound editor for *American Graffiti* asked for R2D2 (Reel 2, Dialogue 2), Lucas made a note in his book for a cool name. When his pal Terry McGovern ran over a small animal while they were driving and said, "I think I just ran over a Wookie back there," Lucas made another note. The Force (energy generated by every living being) was inspired by Carlos Casteneda's cult book classic *Tales of Power*. The bit of the Banthas (remember the hairy elephantine beasts of burden in the desert?) was borrowed from Burroughs' novel, *The Lost World*.

The evil emperor of the Evil Empire seemed to come straight from Flash Gordon's

Emperor Ming the Merciless. Han Solo, the mercenary with a good heart, was plucked from westerns. The alien who threatens Luke in the Cantina scene with the line, "You just watch yourself—we're wanted men. I have the death sentence on twelve systems," followed by Obi-Wan cutting his arm off with a light saber was lifted straight out of Toshiro Mifune's lips in Akira Kurosawa's Japanese western *Yojimbo* (1961). Luke's grievous discovery of his aunt and uncle's slaughter and the destruction of their ranch is a nod to John Ford, John Wayne, and *The Searchers* (1956).

Now to cast the story. Orson Welles as Darth Vader? Toshiro Mifune as Ben? It could have been. Teaming up with director Brian De Palma, who was casting *Carrie* (1976), Lucas saw forty actors a day. Fifty made it to callbacks. Nick Nolte, Jodie Foster, and Amy Irving all fell by the wayside. Final choices trimmed down to three: Will Selzer or Mark Hamill as Luke, Terri Nunn or Carrie Fisher as Leia, and Christopher Walken or Harrison Ford as Han. Will was too sophisticated, former *Penthouse* Pet Terri was too hard, and Walken was too sinister. Word had gone out the *American Graffiti* cast wasn't going to be considered, but Ford (who had played a hot-rodder) ran into Lucas while Ford was doing some carpentry on Coppola's office door. Lucas let Ford read across from possible Leias, and it was the actor's frustration at helping others audition for a movie he was shut out of that won him the role.

Lucas admitted that his biggest challenge was to make *Star Wars* credible: "In order to create this fabricated reality I needed actors who could take fantastic and impossible situations and infuse them with an almost documentary authenticity....I needed Alec Guinness." Sir Alec was in town doing a cameo in *Murder by Death* (1976) when an unsolicited script came over the transom with a kid brandishing a light sword on the cover. *Murder* director Robert Moore had high praise for Lucas's two previous films, so Guinness read it but thought, "Good God, it's science fiction! Why are they offering me this?" Though he found the dialogue "a bit ropey," he was also hooked on the suspense.

BELOW: Darth Vader (the voice of James Earl Jones and the body of David Prowse) reaches out to bring Luke over to the Dark Side in The Empire Strikes Back *(1980). RIGHT:* Flash Gordon, *blond-haired hero (Buster Crabbe at left), and Ming the Merciless (Charles Middleton) could have been prototypes for Luke and Darth.*

Meeting with the writer/director, Guinness admitted he wasn't thrilled with the description of Ben as an "old desert rat." He told Lucas he didn't want to play "some wild, eccentric, half-dotty old man appearing out of a hole in the sand dunes." Lucas likened it to Gandalf the wizard in J.R.R. Tolkien's *Lord of the Rings* and Guinness mused, "Yes, I can do something like that—a quiet character, not too mystical or strange, but sympathetic." Alec was in and off to England as the cast went to film interiors at the Elstree studios where Stanley Kubrick and Alfred Hitchcock had made films. But there was trouble in paradise.

There was no time for rehearsal—not even a read-through. Lucas found that Guinness' role of Ben needed to be killed off halfway through the picture. His role eviscerated, Guinness threatened to walk off the project until Lucas worked in Guinness' disembodied voice as the embodiment of the Force. Carrie Fisher, who was supposed to drop ten pounds (4.5kg) for a role she saw as too pretty for her to play, had to tape her breasts down to achieve a tomboyish figure and say comic-book lines like, "I thought I recognized your foul stench when I was brought on board, Governor Tarkin." Ford was less diplomatic, often taunting Lucas: "You can type this shit, but you sure can't say it." The English crew was

openly derisive about what it saw as a ridiculous script (before any sensational special effects were added) and when Alan Ladd, Jr., visited the set to watch forty minutes of unedited rushes that included bodybuilder Dave Prowse's unintelligible, unsinister voice behind a mask, the movie was almost shut down.

After seventy days in the studio, Lucas took his show on the road to Death Valley and Tunisia to replicate the desert of Luke's home planet. The prefabricated sets took crews four days to move a mere thirty miles (48km) in the desert. The two-story-tall, ninety-foot (27m) long sand crawler was blown apart in a sandstorm. Cast members also had to battle dysentery and freezing nighttime temperatures. While Anthony Daniels braved bruises from the sharp interior edges of his C3P0 costume, three-foot-eight-inch (112cm) tall Kenny Baker could hardly move his R2D2 costume through the sand and was so deaf inside it that grips had to rap on his costume with a hammer to signal action.

Over budget and behind schedule, Lucas came home without time or money to even satisfactorily finish his sleazy Cantina scene filled with aliens of every stripe. What none of the cast or brass knew was the technical virtuosity that would pull the slim yet archetypal story together into a magnificent microcosm. Friend Steven Spielberg introduced Lucas to *Jaws* (1975) composer John Williams, who wrote the now-famous, thundering, Max Steineresque Hollywood score. Where dialogue had sounded corny, it now seemed completely supported and swelled with adventure. The visuals were even richer.

"Designing a universe was very complicated and time-consuming," confessed Lucas. "We couldn't go out to the store and buy things; we had to design everything from the forks and plates to the clothing and binoculars, to all the transportation vehicles and spaceships. You have to figure out communications devices, computers, even panels in a hallway. And everything has to look like it fits." To do so, Lucas enlisted former Boeing aircraft technical illustrator Ralph McQuarrie, created his own special effects studio (Industrial Light and Magic), and made some very strange suggestions.

Could the rebel cruiser's design model really come from the shape of an outboard boat motor? You bet. In the first *Star Wars* sequel, *The Empire Strikes Back* (1980), could Jabba the Hut's slave ship really have been based on the shape of a streetlamp outside Lucas' SFX studio? Oh, yes. Did Solo's Millennium Falcon really end up looking just like Lucas' favorite fast food, the hamburger? Take a look. On these strangely inspired shapes, McQuarrie and builders Johnston and Rodis Romero went to work. Lucas continually pushed for basic designs to look less sleek and more industrial. The Romeros "bashed" hundreds of models, cannibalizing B-29 fuselages, aircraft carrier decks, and motorboat hulls to add detail to their creations. The Empire's seemingly six-mile (10km) long star destroyer that passes overhead as the film opens was actually three feet (91.5cm) long but was filmed almost microscopically with thousands of tiny fiber-optic cables that created windows of light. One model of the Millennium Falcon was no bigger than a quarter.

After all the hardship, after Lucas' minimal (but, Guinness insists, expert) input to the actors, and after all the money was spent, Ladd took one look at Lucas' working print and dumbfoundedly proclaimed to the Fox board of directors that *Star Wars* was "possibly the greatest picture ever made. That's my absolute statement." The thrill was there. The sci-fi serial had joined forces with the western, heroic mythology, coming-of-age quests, and metaphysics to create some of the best and most loving entertainment of all time. By paying tribute to its genre's less-than-glorious legacy, *Star Wars* paved the way for a visionary and big-budgeted future to come, not only in sequels like *The Empire Strikes Back* (1980) and *Return of the Jedi* (1983) but with blockbusters from Steven Spielberg's *E.T. The Extra-Terrestrial* (1982) to David Twohy's *The Arrival* (1996).

As for Lucas, he had originally offered to cut his rights to any profits the film might make by $600,000 in return for control of merchandising. Fox execs must have rubbed their hands with greedy glee at the deal. However, there was still a little left over for Lucas after the film grossed $525 million, and the moguls would have plenty of time to wring their hands as they packed their kids off to school with Darth Vader lunch boxes and off to trick-or-treat in Wookie costumes.

BELOW: Han Solo (Harrison Ford) is welcomed by Lando Calrissian (Billy Dee Williams) to his Cloud City. Lando's warm reception, however, belies a cooler plot in The Empire Strikes Back.

QUAKE IN FEAR, YOU TINY FOOLS!

Scientists are quiet, introverted, self-effacing people, right? Not in the movies, they're not. There's something about knowledge that seems to drive the smartest of them a little crazy. Maybe it has to do with muddling up what man was never meant to meddle in. Part and parcel of being a successful mad scientist has always been the ability to make some pretty outrageous claims. Try these restrained statements of scientific fact on for size. You might want to use one the next time you fix the lawn mower or are slapped with a library fine.

"We have made machines out of men. Now I will make men out of machines!"

 —*Rudolf Klein-Rogge in* **Metropolis** *(1926)*

"Crazy, am I? We'll see whether I'm crazy or not....I have discovered the great ray which first brought life into the world!"

 —*Colin Clive in* **Frankenstein** *(1931)*

"That's what I needed—living flesh from humans for my experiments!"

 —*Lionel Atwill in* **Doctor X** *(1932)*

"Free! Free at last! Ah! Mad, eh, Lanyon? You hypocrites, deniers of life, if you could see me now what would you think?"

 —*Fredric March in* **Dr. Jekyll and Mr. Hyde** *(1932)*

[At being called a "fiend"] "I am a doctor of philosophy from Edinburgh University. I am a doctor of law from Christchurch. I am a doctor of medicine from Harvard. My friends, out of courtesy, call me doctor."

 —*Boris Karloff in* **The Mask of Fu Manchu** *(1932)*

"Do you know what it means to feel like God?"

 —*Charles Laughton in* **Island of Lost Souls** *(1933)*

"We'll soon put the world right now, Kemp. We'll begin with a reign of terror. A few murders here and there. Murders of great men...murders of little men. Just to show that we make no distinction. We might even wreck a train or two."

 —*Claude Rains in* **The Invisible Man** *(1933)*

"Ha! You shudder in horror! So did I the first time...but what are a few lives when weighed in the balance against the achievement of biological science?"

 —*Lionel Atwill in* **The Vampire Bat** *(1933)*

"Small, small, we can make the whole world small!"

 —*Rafaela Ottiano in* **The Devil-Doll** *(1936)*

"I've harnessed it at last, Benet!"

 — *Boris Karloff in* **The Invisible Ray** *(1936)*

"When those you love best lie dying, think back to this moment when you held their salvation in your hands and threw it away. Always remember that I offered you life and you gave me death."

 —*Boris Karloff in* **The Man They Could Not Hang** *(1939)*

"Of course I'm mad, but while you were fooling with conventions, I have conquered destiny....The worker of the future! Electronically alive! Every impulse controlled by me!"

 —*Lionel Atwill in* **Man Made Monster** *(1941)*

"I am prepared to supply my country with a new army, an army that will not need to be fed, that cannot be stopped by bullets, that is in fact invincible—an army of the living dead."

 —*John Carradine in* **Revenge of the Zombies** *(1943)*

"Yes, the neat and unconfused reproductive technique of vegetation. No pain or pleasure as we know it. Superior, our superior in every way."

> —Robert Cornthwaite in The Thing (1951)

"I would put my knife into the brains of a hundred men, a thousand, and destroy them all...if I could restore her to me for only one day."

> —Basil Rathbone in The Black Sleep (1956)

"Ladies and gentlemen, just a word of warning: if you are not convinced that you have a tingler of your own, the next time you're frightened...don't scream."

> —Vincent Price in The Tingler (1959)

"I shall become the inheritor of all my 104 years. Of all the sickness I never had, of every pain, blemish, disease—a lifetime of illness in one moment."

> —Christopher Lee in The Man Who Could Cheat Death (1959)

"No matter how far I take my creatures they begin to revert. They can't tell me what happens inside their bodies when that occurs, until now. You will do that for me. You will explore that inner battlefield, that war of the cells, and bring back the knowledge, the ultimate knowledge to become an animal."

> —Burt Lancaster in The Island of Dr. Moreau (1971)

"Dare I bring such a monstrous creature back to life? What havoc might I wreak on an unsuspecting world? Well...[slaps hands together] we'll take a chance."

> —Gene Wilder in Young Frankenstein (1974)

Experiment in terror. Just one of the scare tactics to rouse enough fear to activate The Tingler (1959) attached to the spine of this helpless mute. No scream means no mercy.

"I'm saying that I don't feel very human anymore. I'm saying I'm an insect who dreamt he was a man and loved it, but now the dream is over, and the insect is awake. I'm saying I'll hurt you if you stay."

> —Jeff Goldblum in The Fly (1986)

"We've experienced death. Somehow we've brought our sins back with us...and they're pissed."

> —Kiefer Sutherland in Flatliners (1990)

Chapter Two

TAKE US TO YOUR MOVIES

The appearance of the wheels and their work was like unto the colour of a beryl [a seagreen gemstone]: and they four had one likeness: and their appearance and their work was as if it were a wheel in the middle of a wheel....And when the living creatures went, the wheels went by them: and when the living creatures were lifted from Earth, the wheels were lifted up.

—Ezekiel 1-16, which some cite as an early account of alien abduction

If the Martian fighting machines don't look exactly like the towering tripods from H.G. Wells' novel, that's o.k.; these creations for George Pal's War of the Worlds (1953) are plenty scary and très modern.

THE POWER OF PULP!

We are not alone. Words of comfort to some and terror to others, but to many minds in science they are words of certainty. Our little globe is, after all, but a speck in a sea of other stars. In January 1996 the radiotelescope discovery of planets orbiting star 47 (Ursae), star 51 (Pegasi), and star 70 (Virginis) made it pretty clear that the billions of stars in the universe must have zillions of planets. In August of that year, scientists at Stanford University and NASA's Johnson Space Center announced an earthshaking find about our planetary neighbor Mars. After placing a fragment of a Martian asteroid, discovered in the Antarctic in 1984, into a laser bombardment chamber, not only did hydrocarbon molecules indicate former bacterial life in the rock, but tiny tubular shapes found may be fossils of ancient Martian life.

Can we really be so stuck on ourselves as to believe that we are the only intelligent life-form on the cosmic block? Government-funded projects suggest otherwise. Since the 1960s, S.E.T.I. (Search for Extraterrestrial Intelligence) radio astronomy projects have been enough of a reality that *The Arrival* (1996) arrived with horri-

ABOVE: It's a race against time in the desert to stop alien world domination for Charlie Sheen and Teri Poco in The Arrival.

ble aliens, a paranoid plot, and a bearded Charlie Sheen. Most folks know the questions that arose from Hangar 18 or what Project Blue Book was. In fact, one out of every four U.S. citizens reports having seen something in the skies that defies explanation. (This even applies to your author who, one summer afternoon when he was twelve, stood with his entire family as a gleaming, featureless capsule arced its way across the western Maine sky, only to have the local Air Force base draw a blank on any satellites in the area.) As Fox Mulder insists in the popular TV fare *X-Files*, "The truth is out there." Well, the truth, or something else just as out there, has been in books for more than a hundred years now.

By the 1860s, former law student Jules Verne was writing on travel by every amazing means of locomotion imaginable—from a hot-air balloon (hundreds of them) to a submarine to a rocket to the moon to a machine burrowing into the center of the earth. By the late 1890s, on the other side of the English Channel, Herbert George Wells, who would turn his hand to so many kinds of writing (including the most respected survey of world history ever written), was crafting more harrowing, speculative works about mad scientists making themselves invisible, time travelers, futuristic societies, and, yes, invaders from outer space.

Science fiction had been fathered, and in England, the cradle was soon rocked by a number of hands. Illustrated magazines like *The Strand*, *The Windsor*, *Pearson's*, *Cassell's*, and *The Idler* were filled with pseudoscientific flights of Victorian fancy. As Charles Dickens had done so deftly before them, Wells (*In the Avu Observatory* and countless other short stories) and Wellsian acolytes like E. Tickner-Edwardes (*The Man Who Meddled With Eternity: The Result of a Terrible Experiment*), George C. Wallis (*The Last Days of Earth: Being the Story of the Launching of the Red Sphere*), Fred M. White (*The Dust of Death: The Story of the Great Plague of the Twentieth Century*), George Griffith (*From Pole to Pole: An Account of a Journey Through the Axis of the Earth, Collated From the Diaries of the Late Professor Hafkin and his Niece Mrs. Arthur Princeps*), and E.E. Kellett (*The Lady Automaton*) thrilled turn-of-the-century readers in monthly installments of imagination lovingly illustrated.

The cradle rocked even faster across the Atlantic when Luxemborgian-born and -educated amateur scientist and sometimes writer Hugo Gernsback came to the United States and, after starting a magazine devoted to radio technology (*Modern Electrics*), tried his hand at something a little riskier. *Argosy* (established in 1882) had brought respected fantasist James Branch Cabell and his stories of the mythical kingdom of Poictesme to a larger reading public, as *All-Story* (established in 1914) had swung Tarzan creator Edgar Rice Burroughs into view. But Gernsback wanted to create a magazine forum for what he called "scientifiction." *Amazing Stories* was created to publish stories "based on science that would interest young men in scientific careers." To that end the superlative writings of Wells, Verne, and other Victorians were showcased.

Other "pulp" magazines (named for their inexpensive pulp-wood paper) such as *Astounding Stories*, *Thrilling Wonder Stories*, and *Weird Tales* also followed Gernsback's lead and garnered legions of loyal fans, introducing the work of American writers like the great H.P. Lovecraft (*The Colour Out of Space*) and influencing generations of science fiction and horror writers to come. These magazines also paid writers a pretty penny. Luckily, as "space opera" (adventures of folks like Flash Gordon to other planets complete with shapely Martian damsels in distress) took over more and more of the magazines' content, another transformation took place.

In 1937, a writer named John W. Campbell, Jr., took over *Astounding Stories* and changed its name to *Astounding Science Fiction*. His new mag focused not on gadgetry and technology riddled boys' adventure, but on stories conceptualizing the often frightening societal implications of technological advances. In other words, this was science fiction for grown-ups. To do this he recruited and nurtured unknown young men of science and literature whose names would one day become legendary: Isaac Asimov, Arthur C. Clarke, Robert Heinlein, A.E. Van Gogt, and Theodore Sturgeon, to name a few. Their stories were so visionary (like Campbell's own *The Space Beyond*, which centered on the horrific possibilities of a nuclear chain reaction) that he was investigated by the FBI.

Within a year of the atomic devastation of Hiroshima and Nagasaki, the reading public had a newfound respect for, and perhaps a nervous interest in, science fiction. It wasn't fluff for eggheads and kids anymore. By 1946 Random House had published its first hardcover science fiction anthology. By 1949 Doubleday was in with a line of science fiction novels in hardcover. By 1950, pulp science fiction mags had proliferated from eight to twenty. One story from one such magazine, written by the editor of *Astounding Science Fiction* himself, would become one of the best science fiction films ever made.

shifter of the story. What one character calls "an intellectual carrot" is *The Thing (from Another World)* (1951), a hulking, more than seven-foot (213cm) tall creature who thrives on human blood, whose vegoid body is regenerative and impervious to gunfire, whose strength is colossal, whose thorn-covered arms are veritable cleavers, and whose seedlings can grow (if fed with the proper amount of plasma) at an alarming rate. With the human inhabitants of the army outpost locked in against the Arctic night, the Thing (defrosted when a squeamish soldier guarding the block of ice that the creature was frozen in throws a blanket over its ugliness—an electric blanket!) is out in the swirling snow, gutting huskies and preparing for an all-out assault on his first human morsels; this script had real fear potential.

The first draft of the screenplay endowed the space creature with "stringy-looking fingers," "multiple eyes," and a "bulbous head." Only the bulbous head stayed. After eighteen prototypes, what makeup designer Lee Greenway came up with for one of filmdom's first space creatures was a one-piece prosthetic that fit over the actor's nose and cheekbones, around his ears, down his neck, and over his forehead. Veins ran across the surface of the makeup and attached to football bladders strapped to the chest, as did ventilation tubes under the makeup. This way, the actor's breathing not only cooled his buried face and swelled his bulging forehead but also pumped multicolored blood through the veins visible on top of it.

I COME IN PEACE—YOU COME IN PIECES

With former World War II allies the Russians now turned creepy communists, the American public of the early 1950s was feeling pretty edgy. They were increasingly fearful and fascinated by stories of the evils of technology and the peril of invasion. American movie director Howard Hawks had read a real humdinger of an invasion story in a science fiction magazine he picked up at the Army PX in Heidelberg, Germany, where he was filming the Cary Grant comedy *I Was a Male War Bride* (1949). The 1938 short story was called "Who Goes There?" and the author was John W. Campbell, Jr.

Campbell's story detailed an Arctic expedition investigating a huge object imbedded in the ice after what appeared to be a meteor crash. It isn't a meteor, of course, but a spaceship. And the frozen body they retrieve isn't E.T., of course, but a creature sent here to colonize, and, yes, take over the earth. It can change shape at will. It can assume the shape and even the manner of its next host (before of course destroying it in a hideous mutation). It can read minds and project its thoughts. And it has the ability to squeeze through cracks a rat would need dieting to try. There is no stopping it.

What Hawks was interested in was the first four pages, roughly the discovery of an alien creature in a brutal, alien yet terrestrial environment. He purchased the story for $900 and paid writers Ben Hecht and Charles Lederer $10,000 a week apiece to write a script about a creature more in the Frankenstein mold than the shape-

If this man looks terrified, it's because he is. Trapped in an arctic experimental station, he and his cohorts have thawed out **The Thing (from Another World)** *(1950) and now it's open season on humans.*

Six-foot-five-inch (226cm) tall (plus four-inch [10cm] lifts) James Arness ate every meal on the set in an attempt to keep word of the monstrous makeup from leaking to the movie public. Yet special effects were hardly key here. This is one alien creature movie where the fear is implied rather than impaled. The Thing itself is seen only fleetingly until the electrifying climax, but the carefully crafted suspense and paranoia (the besieged humans can anticipate the Thing's presence by their Geiger counters) leading up to each encounter make it truly terrifying. While we hear the Thing's roar (a cat howl slowed down and amplified), we only hear about its seedlings mewling "almost like the wail of a newborn child that's hungry" or the crew members found in the greenhouse hung upside down, slaughterhouse-style. Special effects of the Thing burning its way through an iron wall or decapitating a scientist were cut and focus was given to more basic elements.

Expert ensemble acting and writing in a monster movie? You bet. From four hundred interviews and seventy screen tests, producer Hawks and neophyte director Christian Nyby (Hawks valued Nyby's editing on *Red River*, 1948, so much that he vowed to get Nyby a film to direct) pulled a great many of their players from the world of radio who all handled the Hawksian style of rapid fire, overlapping dialogue as deftly as Cary Grant, Carole Lombard, or Humphrey Bogart ever did.

The beginning of each shooting day found the actors sitting around a table and working copious ad-libs into the day's dialogue. When the Air Force refused assistance on the film because their manual said, "There is no such thing as a flying saucer," Hawks ironically quoted Bulletin 629, Item 6700, Extract 75131 chapter and verse in its assessment of the phenomena as being due to 1) misinterpretation, 2) mass hysteria, or 3) jokes. With material this fresh and glib and unusually credible performances, the film is a joy to watch.

The wonderfully aloof and low-key Robert Cornthwaite, who had been a radio linguist and dialectician, was perfect for the insanely idealistic Professor Carrington. Kenneth Tobey (Captain Douglas Spencer) and Margaret Sheridan (a scientist named Nikki) are old flames who communicate both their fear and desire in crackling army banter (though their big kissing scene was edited out). Benefiting from what he called "next-door nepotism," Nyby's neighbor, radio-voice George Fenneman (later Groucho's TV sidekick on *You Bet Your Life*), was signed on for a week's work that became fourteen. None in the company earned more than $800 a week. The lion's share of Hawks' budget dollars went to making the film as realistic as possible.

The California Institue of Technology rented out $500,000 worth of real scientific equipment for the ersatz Arctic lab. The original exterior shooting location of Cutbank, Montana, was so devoid of snow that a nineteen-week wait produced little more than the overhead shot of the army plane circling the spaceship buried beneath the ice (if you keep your eyes open you can glimpse the dots of a horse and men clearing the ice). Ice fields made of salt, tempered masonite, and photographic solution (for sheen) were set up at the RKO Ranch in the San Fernando Valley.

The temperatures were hardly polar. The up-to-100°F (38°C) heat was sweltering enough to send saltwater rivulets into nearby orchards. "It was terrible," bemoaned cast member Dewey Martin. "We had to wear those huge parkas, the lined jobs. They were using plastic and cornflakes for snow, and they had these big wind machines blowing it in our faces...and we were so hot and sweaty that this crap would stick to our faces, and it would get down in the neckline, and down into our heavy underwear. I'm telling you it was rough." To do the frosty interiors, Hawks, Nyby, and company resorted to local Los Angeles icehouses. Even so, the actors had to tank up on hot cocoa and coffee all day long to keep their breath as hot and visible as possible. "Of course, we were all going to the can all day long," Tobey added.

OPPOSITE: No, that's not "Son of Thing" perched behind the much made-up mystery star of The Thing (from Another World) (1950), just a special-effects actor for the film's electrifying finale. ABOVE: A bearded and frosted Kurt Russell indulges in a paranoiac pow-wow with crew mates who may or may not be aliens in in John Carpenter's chilling remake of The Thing (1982).

One trooper who didn't grumble was director Christian Nyby, who has been stripped of directorial credit over the years by the assumption (not unlike the one that Tobe Hooper produced and Steven Spielberg directed *Poltergeist*, 1982) that Hawks really directed. The truth is that Hawks helped before Nyby set about working his editing magic, for as Nyby admitted, "When you're being taught to paint by Rembrandt, you don't take the brush out of his hand." The truth is it doesn't matter. What does is how creepy this film still is—creepy enough to cause one woman in the Pasadena preview audience to faint (which Nyby admitted "delighted" him), creepy enough to be the "first movie that made me jump out of my seat—literally," according to future horror and sci-fi master John Carpenter.

Carpenter liked it so much that in 1982 he made a stunningly grisly, paranoiac remake of his own. With its incredible special effects, it was able to adhere more faithfully to Campbell's original story while lacking the scary simplicity of the original, whose paranoiac last words of warning broadcast from the frozen wastes still chill a nation of moviegoers: "Watch the skies, everywhere, keep looking, keep watching the skies!"

WITH A LITTLE HELP FROM OUR FRIENDS (IF WE DON'T KILL THEM)

Not everyone was "watching the skies" with their hand on their holster.

In the same year as Hawks' *The Thing (from Another World)*, Robert Wise, the equally skilled director of films as diverse as *The Curse of the Cat People* (1944), *Run Silent, Run Deep* (1958), *West Side Story* (1961), *The Haunting* (1963), and *The Sound of Music* (1965) adapted a short story by Harry Bates into one of the best and most meaningful science fiction movies of all time, *The Day the Earth Stood Still* (1951).

Bates had sold his 1940 story *Farewell to the Master* to Paramount for $1,000 ($500 of which was snatched up by his publisher). The story told of Klaatu, an emissary from another world who lands his huge flying disc in Washington, D.C. With a twelve-foot (3.5m) tall robot capable of unlimited destruction named Gnut at his side, the Christlike Klaatu tries to communicate to a very hostile reception party of earthlings that their planet's nuclear

> *"Out stepped a man, god-like in appearance and human in form. The first thing he did was to raise his right arm high in the universal gesture of peace; but it was not that which impressed those nearest so much as the expression on his face, which radiated kindness, wisdom, the purest nobility. In his delicately tinted robe he looked like a benign god."*
>
> **—a description of Klaatu from Harry Bates' story *Farewell to the Master***

warfare and technology will soon expand out into space and that other worlds, which have vanquished aggression, will not tolerate the spreading violence. Earth will be destroyed if it stays on its destructive course. Unfortunately, Klaatu is shot before he can complete his mission, and despite Gnut's efforts to clone him, his warning is never fully completed. One newspaperman who tries to help the robot back aboard the airship asks Gnut to tell its masters that the people of Earth are sorry for killing Klaatu. Gnut replies, "You misunderstand. I am the master."

Wise dropped the twist ending but fleshed out the script thanks to Edmund North. Klaatu and (now) Gort would land in D.C., and after emerging from the seemingly hermetically sealed craft, Klaatu would be shot offering a gift for the American president. In response the huge Gort evaporates field artillery and soldiers' rifles before any more damage can be done. Klaatu is whisked away and treated in Washington's Walter Reade hospital. There, recovering uncannily quickly, he learns from the president's secretary of the political impossibility of gathering the heads of all Earth's nations to deliver his message. So Klaatu slips past security to mingle with Earth's inhabitants to find out what makes them so bellicose.

As a manhunt begins for the missing "menacing" alien, Klaatu takes a room at a local boarding house (thanks to a soldier's dry cleaning, wallet, and suitcase that he has borrowed). He meets a widow, Helen Benson, and her son, Bobby. The boy's openness and intelligence, a sharp contrast to the other fearful and prejudiced tenants, impresses the wise and impeccably polite alien. Through Bobby he learns of the country's leading scientist, Dr. Barnhardt, whom Klaatu convinces that he is indeed from another planet by correctly finishing a chalkboard-wide equation in celestial navigation that the doctor has been agonizing over for months.

Through the doctor, Klaatu hopes to at least reach a congregation of the world's finest minds, but Barnhardt believes a show of power will be necessary to convince them. Klaatu devises a plan to stop all electricity across the entire globe for half an hour (except of course for things like hospitals and planes). That muscle may impress the eggheads, but the military meatheads just want him exterminated. A dragnet closes in around Klaatu and the one earthling he has fully confided in, Helen Benson.

LEFT: Patricia Neal doesn't know that Gort the super-robot just wants to help her up in **The Day the Earth Stood Still (1951). OPPOSITE: With Klaatu (Michael Rennie) at her side she's a lot calmer.**

While other movies filled with melodrama and creaky special effects look like little more than camp now, the lean, mean story and impeccable direction make *The Day the Earth Stood Still* an unforgettable classic. Wise, who edited *Citizen Kane* (1941), knew how to make movies move. From the first nanoseconds of Klaatu's craft's landing, the documentarian quickly cuts between action and shots of an awestruck, paranoiac public. The assembly of two hundred extras as National Guardsmen (the Defense Department wouldn't help out a pacifist film during the Korean conflict) surrounding the saucer in bustling, downtown D.C. look real. The montage of vile broadcasts and public alarm when Klaatu escapes makes things even more conceivable.

Composer Bernard Herrmann's edgy score creates another level of urgency. Given free rein, the maestro of films from *Psycho* (1960) to *Taxi Driver* (1976) used an electric violin, an electric bass, four harps, four pianos, thirty brass members, and two theremins plus an occasional hot-water bottle and a vibraphone played in reverse for the chilling electrical standstill.

The acting is stellarly underplayed. Though Claude Rains was initially considered, celebrated British film star Michael Rennie, with his ectomorphic physique, angular face, and calm, otherworldly intensity, is a little more than human yet less than godlike and therefore perfect. The former flight instructor wryly admitted that he may have been picked for this character (which by the end of his career would be his favorite) because "Hollywood moviemakers apparently thought I was odd enough looking to have come from anywhere in the universe." He looks good in the one-piece space suit that designer Perkins Bailey made for him, which was cool enough to hit the men's fashion circuit even before the film was released.

The towering man of liquid metal is just as cool. Who would have thought that beneath the shining skin of the twelve-foot (3.5m) tall, single-eyed, lethally armed robot Gort was the seven-foot-seven-inch (231cm) tall Lock Martin, doorman at Hollywood's famed Grauman's Chinese Theater? Martin wore two rubber costumes (one that zipped up the front and one that zipped up the back, of course) that would suffocate his skin if he was left in them for more than forty-five minutes. As he was not a particularly strong man, a crane was needed to help him carry Helen Benson (a delightfully unhysterical Patricia Neal) at the film's climax.

Neal, herself one of the best actresses of her generation, has just the right mix of skepticism, attraction, and fear in meeting a being from another world on a desperate and potentially deadly mission. She only had trouble spitting out the immortal mouthful that science fiction film fans the world over have come to know: "Klaatu barada nikto."

Previously directing *The Curse of the Cat People* (1944) under thinking man's horror producer Val Lewton had taught Wise the value of believability and atmosphere. "Instead of depending entirely on the horror aspects of such a visitor," Wise noted, "producer Julian Blaustein and I insisted that the story make sense." Even so, the effects here are impressive. The spaceship, a $100,000,

350-foot (107m) wide, twenty-five-foot (7.5m) tall frame of plywood covered with plaster of paris really did take off (for a few seconds before crashing) thanks to the winds on the Twentieth Century Fox lot. The sliding front door is invisible until opened thanks to edges coated with soft plastic and repainted silver for every shot. The just-as-mafically-sealed-looking dome splitting open and sliding out a vast metalic ramp is also an eerily smooth effect which would be copied in countless films to come. The less-is-more ship interior is a trendsetter, too, with its lucite parts, corrugated glass walls, seemingly heat-sensitive controls, and big bubble in the center.

Other quasibenevolent visitors would come during the decade. In a crater built fifteen miles (24km) north of Hollywood (though it's supposed to be Sand Rock, Arizona), *It Came from Outer Space* (1953) was filmed. Jack Arnold's 3-D story of "xenomorphs" involves creatures that take over human bodies (making their eyes glow), but only because they want to get their spaceship (a huge, geodesic dome) back into outer space. And what they really look like is a "fried egg." In Joseph Newman's *This Island Earth* (1954), white-haired aliens with bulging skulls kidnap scientists to save civilization on the planet Metaluna, but send them back home in the end. No one ever again tries to come to our planet to save us from ourselves. Klaatu, we miss you!

BLAST OFF!

Rocket ships didn't seem so silly after World War II. Not with the German V-1 buzz bombs raining death over London during the summer of 1944 and the much more powerful secret weapon, the V-2 rocket, launched after the Normandy invasion. Still, though depicted with surprising realism by Fritz Lang in his By *Rocket to the Moon* (1929), it wasn't until 1950 that movie rockets really blasted off with audiences.

ABOVE: *When my baby smiles at me, I invade Rio. Martians lay waste to Brazil's sun and fun city in* The War of the Worlds.

Rocket Ship X-M (1950) landed on Mars to find killer mutants roaming around after atomic devastation, and much better fare still was science fiction film pioneer George Pal's Destination Moon (1950). The thrill of a moon landing may be passé now, but the pointy ship and bubble helmets on the astronauts set the tone for countless space films to come.

Pal, who was born in Budapest in 1908, worked as a set designer and animator in Berlin until he fled from the Nazis. His expertise in stop-motion puppet films (an inspiration for future endeavors from Gumby to Tim Burton's The Nightmare Before Christmas, 1993) got Paramount's attention. But only after his Special Effects Oscar for Destination Moon did they consent to

back his second film, about an exodus from Earth during the planet's collision course with another planet, When Worlds Collide (1951). He won another Special Effects Oscar for the film, and it helped give him the opportunity to put on the screen one of the greatest science fiction novels of all time, H.G. Wells' The War of the Worlds (1953).

Paramount had owned the film rights to the 1898 novel since 1927. Orson Welles' Halloween 1938 radio broadcast of Howard Koch's modern Americanization of the story (where the sound of the Martian cylinder unscrewing was reportedly accomplished by opening a pickle jar in a toilet bowl) and the mass hysteria that ensued interested the studio even more. Pal was given a big budget for special effects. Three months went into filming live-action sequences where Cal Tech scientist Dr. Clayton Forrester (Gene Barry) and future librarian Sylvia Van Buren (Ann Robinson) witness Martian fighting machines that emerge from supposed meteors near Linda Rosa, California, and proceed to defeat the police, the army, and even the atomic bomb (which required an in-studio blast more than seventy-five feet [23m] high) on their way to laying waste to Los Angeles before being tackled by an earth ally they would never have imagined. A solid year went into postproduction special effects.

Starting with a 2½-minute tour of Mars and other nearby planets eerily narrated by Sir Cedric Hardwicke, the film also used thousands of hand-painted frames (military artillery being dissolved by a Martian heat ray required four thousand frames while a soldier's dissolution to a skeleton and then dust took only 140) and a process of optical printing whereby up to twenty-four different exposures could be superimposed onto one frame of film.

Designer Al Nozaki totally revamped the Martian war machine of the book (a huge saucer on a towering metal tripod) into something resembling a manta ray. Though they looked immense, models were only forty-two inches (107cm) across and twenty-two inches (56cm) high. They were wrapped in red foil and controlled by more than twelve wires. The killing eye on its stalklike antenna was only ten feet (3m) long and looked suspiciously like the lens of a projection television. A rotary fan in front of a light bulb created the pulse of the laser blast. An electric guitar recording played backward provided the sound.

With solid performances (especially from Barry), a credible script, incredible footage of Martian invaders running amok in Los Angeles (as well as later shots of dead Martians in international locales), and even a sneak peak at the Northrop Flying Wing (precursor to the Stealth bomber and shelved alternative to the B-52),

ABOVE: Not to give anything away, but that three-fingered martian hand isn't coming out to grasp a victory wreath as Gene Barry et al slowly advance through wrecked Los Angeles. RIGHT: Just small town folks confronted by a paranoid nightmare: Becky, Jack, Theodora, and Dr. Miles Bennell have met the enemy...and he is us, in Don Siegel's original Invasion of the Body Snatchers (1956).

Pal scored a box-office bull's-eye. Science fiction's preeminent producer made rockets and saucers a science fiction staple during the fifties and by the end of the decade would wow audiences with another H.G. Wells classic he directed, perhaps the best film he ever produced, *The Time Machine* (1960).

WE HAVE MET THE ENEMY AND HE IS US

The worry about a terrestrial invasion swelled into paranoia sometime during 1950 as loose cannon and Wisconsin senator Joseph McCarthy began a four-year reign of terror, accusing the State Department, the Truman and Eisenhower administrations, countless entertainers, and even the U.S. Army of being riddled with card-carrying members of the communist party. Lives were destroyed and xenophobia took on a whole new color—red.

We'd been worried before. As early as 1916, D.W. Griffith's film *The Flying Torpedo* told of the high-tech (for 1916, that is) invasion of California by an Asian enemy. Pearl Harbor gave that fear enough of a factual basis to sweep the West Coast with fear and loathing. The hideous experiments of Nazi doctors like Joseph Mengele made the vivisections of Dr. Moreau seem like child's play. But the "red menace" was even worse than "the yellow peril" or "the Hun." You couldn't lash out at a whole race of people (as Americans had when they herded 100,000 Japanese-Americans into camps during World War II) but had to content yourself with wondering just which of your friends might be a secret member of a sinister, communist cell. Even that term sounded somehow inhuman.

Radar, developed during the war, bounced its first sound

waves off the moon in 1946. The unprecedented power of Mount Palomar's Hale telescope brought the planets even closer with photographs in 1948. With a tangible enemy absent from Senator McCarthy's alluded-to lists, filmmakers gave the public menaces from beyond to play on political fears or disparage them. *The Blob* (1958) literally subsumed earthlings into its hungry, glutinous mass until a fine young American named Steve McQueen stopped it. In the sixties, television's *The Invaders* made our nemesis look just like us. *Village of the Damned* (1960) made tow-headed tots (whose brains look big because their wigs are too small) the villains. But the best friend paranoia ever had was Don Siegel's low-budget (shot in nineteen days for less than $300,000), high-tension (the original ending was so upsetting to preview audiences that it had to be softened) nightmare *Invasion of the Body Snatchers* (1956).

Jack Finney's 1955 book of paranoia and sleeping menaces, *The Body Snatchers*, serialized in *Colliers* magazine and read by producer Walter Wanger, should catch Siegel's

> *"This is probably my best film. I think the world is populated by pods and I wanted to show them."*
>
> **—Don Siegel, director of *Invasion of the Body Snatchers* (1956)**

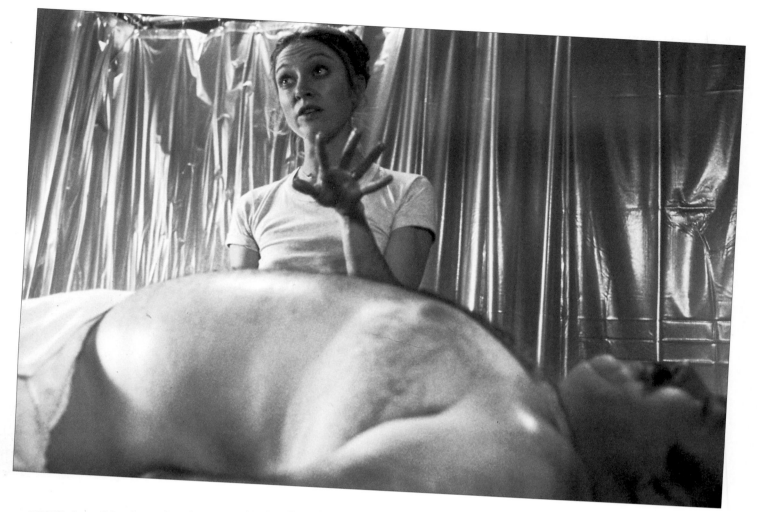

ABOVE: Something funny is going on at this San Francisco spa and Veronica Cartwright doesn't like it one bit in Philip Kaufman's excellent remake of Invasion of the Body Snatchers **(1978).**

reddened eye. The psychological science fiction told of Dr. Miles Bennell returning to the small California town of Santa Mira (the film would actually be shot in the town of Sierra Madre) after a business trip only to find everything more than a little odd.

Folks have been stacking up in his office complaining not about their own health, but that their friends and relatives are somehow imposters. Just driving home, the doc almost runs over a hysterical little boy fleeing from his mother. And yet, Bennell finds that many of these same people are next inexplicably canceling their appointments. The local shrink, Danny Kaufman, calmly writes it off as a kind of mass hysteria, but when Miles' old flame, Becky Driscoll, shows up concerned about a distraught cousin he gets personally involved.

When Miles' good friends, Jack and Theodora Belicec, find something nasty stretched out on their pool table—something that looks like a not-quite-formed Jack clone, something that seems to get more developed every time Jack shuts his eyes—the nightmare begins. Pods from another galaxy have drifted to Earth with the clear intention of replacing the human population, insidiously, unstoppably. And while Miles and Becky intend to hunt down these inhuman impostors, the hunters are very quickly going to become the hunted.

The bland-faced evil in this movie is so diffuse and increasingly pervasive that it's tough not to be sucked in by the fear of it. The scenes in broad daylight of former humans methodically going about the process of distributing pods to take over the human race are terrifying for all their mundanity. Even the affectless aliens' seemingly "benevolent" temperament, when inducing Miles to give up and give in, seems only to obscure a much, much deeper evil. As one of Bennell's formerly trusted friends (and we won't say which one) finally preaches:

> Less than a month ago, Santa Mira was like any other town. People with nothing but problems. Then out of the sky came a solution. Seeds drifting through space for years took root in a farmer's field. From the seeds came pods which had the power to reproduce themselves in the exact likeness of any form of life. Your new bodies are growing in there. They're taking you over cell for cell, atom for atom. There's no pain. Suddenly, while you're asleep, they'll absorb your minds, your memories, and you're reborn into an untroubled world. Tomorrow you'll be one of us. There's no need for love. Love, desire, ambition, faith—without them life is so simple, believe me.

Cuh-ree-pee! Unlike other technology-loving science fiction films of the decade, no scientific part of this process is even vaguely hinted at—nor is it needed. Kevin McCarthy, the clean-cut, vaguely smug, martini-drinking, sleep-deprived, unraveling hero

Miles Bennell, wanted to give the film the Shakespearean title *Sleep No More*. Whatever the pods' mechanics, the moment you finally fall asleep, they've got ya!

Costing less than $15,000 to create, special effects designer Ted Hayworth came up with full-size models of clay for the pods and latex skins over mechanized frames for the "embryo blanks" inside. With simple hydraulic pumps to make them "breathe" and ooze a disgusting, frothy substance, the result was so effective that when Siegel secretly snuck one under Dana Wynter's (Becky Driscoll) hotel-room bed, the actress almost passed out from fright.

Though Allied Artists deleted much of the humor that Siegel and screenwriter Daniel Mainwaring put into their adaptation of Finney's novel, much of the script remained intact. A studio exec objected to the near-nudity of the creatures in the developing pods. Though Hayworth was ready to change his design, Siegel insisted that the exec in question "looked sleepy" and was about to become a pod, and so would raise no objections if they secretly went ahead with their concept. He didn't. Instead of the book's optimistic ending, which had Miles and Becky setting a field of pods afire causing the rest to fly back up into space, Siegel and Mainwaring kept the tension mounting through a terrifying chase and a terrifying kiss that will haunt your dreams...should you let yourself fall asleep.

If by the end of the movie McCarthy looks exhausted as he weaves through traffic, it's because he is. Police allowed Siegel's crew and fifty stunt drivers on an unused cross-bridge off the Hollywood freeway, but only in the wee hours of the morning. But the sequence of the lone, fugitive Bennell hysterically screaming, "You're next! You're next!" right into the camera after he had found a truckload of pods was too much for preview audiences. Allied Artists demanded a more upbeat ending.

Rather than letting studio hacks rework his film, Siegel and Mainwaring decided to create a scene of Bennell in a hospital telling his tale to a skeptical psychiatrist when a highway fatality involving a truckload of pods makes his paranoia suddenly seem chillingly plausible. Sam Peckinpah (who plays the gas meter reader in the film) added narration for McCarthy to wrap it all up.

It's a bit ironic that *Invasion of the Body Snatchers* was taken up as a message film by two opposing political groups. McCarthyites admired it for its oh-so-subtle attack on communist infiltration while, perhaps more perceptively, leftists saw it as a warning against conformity with the conservative majority. The truth was that Siegel had it out for dollar-motivated producers, but left, right, or center, the film went straight for the psychic jugular. Remade twice (the 1978 version featured McCarthy staggering through traffic and Siegel himself as a cabbie), it would be one of the few times that Hollywood would ever touch such a deep nerve of fear with such a minimum of special effects—proof that the best in science fiction doesn't have to be high-tech to give you high blood pressure.

THE POEM FROM OUTER SPACE

Walter Tevis had written the original book from which Hollywood's great, dark, pool-shooting movie *The Hustler* (1961) was adapted. Nevertheless, his science fiction novel of a visitor from a drought-strangled planet coming to Earth to transport water back to his dying family and race, only to become enmeshed in a web of human weaknesses, corruption, and corporate greed, had been turned down as a movie of the week, a television pilot, and a feature (though it was one of the books we saw burned in *Fahrenheit 451*, 1967). Then director Nicolas Roeg (who oddly enough had been the cameraman on *Fahrenheit 451*) got his hot hands on it.

"What drew me to *The Man Who Fell to Earth*," says Roeg, "was that it was a real story that happened to a friend of mine." Roeg's alien friend was a former member of the Egyptian army, who had fled the country after King Farouk had been overthrown. Leaving his wife and children behind, he came to America, living in poverty in New York until landing an accountant's job. Then life overtook him. Working towards his family's passage stretched to seven years and another woman entered his life. When he was tracked down by his wife and begged by her to finally bring his family over, he made his decision. "The night before his family arrived in America he left the woman," says Roeg, "and the pain he went through was incredible."

Strange rationale for a film about an extraterrestrial but the seventies were strange times for film. Science fiction movies of the sixties had started out with a nuclear nightmare called *The Day the Earth Caught Fire* (1962) and the mundane tale of killer weeds from outer space, *The Day of the Triffids* (1963). By mid-decade they had evolved into scenarios as novel as the submarine saga inside the human body, *Fantastic Voyage* (1966), and the trip into the totalitarian, book-burning future, *Fahrenheit 451*. By the close of the sixties, science fiction could be as cartoonishly nutty as Jane Fonda's portrayal of the playmate of the month in outer space, the libidinous *Barbarella* (1968), or as enigmatically elegant as Stanley Kubrick's incredible *2001: a Space Odyssey* (1968). The seventies were ready for a little mellowing.

Aliens didn't have to be such bad folks after all. They could be benign and invisible, encouraging human zoological specimens to

"In Bruegel's 'Icarus' ... everything turns away quite leisurely from the disaster; the ploughman may have heard the splash, the forsaken cry, but for him it was not an important failure; the sun shone, as it had, on the white legs disappearing into the green water; and the expensive delicate ship that must have seen something amazing—a boy falling out of the sky —had somewhere to get to and sailed calmly on."

—poet W.H. Auden on painter Peter Bruegel's *Icarus*, an image central to Nicolas Roeg's visionary *The Man Who Fell to Earth* (1976)

ABOVE: Hot property? One of the books that futuristic fireman Montag (Oskar Werner) and his cronies are about to incinerate in **Fahrenheit 451** (1966) might just be Walter Tevis' **The Man Who Fell to Earth.** BELOW: The man unmasked: David Bowie's true and slightly feline form in **The Man Who Fell to Earth** (1976).

copulate, as the Tralfamadorians had with porn actress Montana Wildhack (Valerie Perrine) and time-tripper Billy Pilgrim (Michael Sacks) in the film of Kurt Vonnegut's *Slaughterhouse-Five* (1972). They could benevolently materialize as our deceased loved ones, as in Andrei Tarkovsky's adaptation of Stanislaw Lem's story *Solaris* (1972). They could be highly intelligent and overlooked mammals as they were in *The Day of the Dolphin* (1973), or they could be cute enough to take on board as pets (after you had decimated their planet) in John Carpenter's stab at Star Trek nobility, *Dark Star* (1974). They could be hot-hot-hot like the emperor Wang, aiming his sex-ray at Earth from the planet Porno in the sex-laden serial spoof *Flesh Gordon* (1974). They could reach for humanity's hand to elevate the species as in *Close Encounters of the Third Kind* (1977) or they could save our hides as in *Superman* (1978).

Why not have an alien we could really relate to, someone almost like us or who would become so? Roeg had adapted Daphne du Maurier's story of fate and clairvoyance into one of the most sensual, cerebral, and classy occult thrillers ever, *Don't Look Now* (1973). Why not bring a little of the same almost poetic mystique to sci-fi? Though Peter O'Toole was the first contender, seeing David Bowie's Cracked Actor video convinced Roeg that the rock star's androgynous, steely yet vulnerable persona was perfect for the protagonist of his kaleidoscopic sojourn. But just how cracked could this actor be?

The alien (a.k.a. Thomas Jerome Newton) would have to make his way quite believably. First, he would sell an abundant supply of inscribed gold rings from desert town to desert town. Next, he would accumulate enough money to hire stellar lawyer Oliver Farnsworth (deftly played by Buck Henry) to register nine basic patents. With an advanced technological lock on ideas like film that develops in the roll, Newton's World Enterprises would make him one of the wealthiest, yet most reclusive, beings on the planet. Still, the tycoon's long-term plan to build a water-bearing rocket would go terrible awry.

His only intimates (his identity is secret even to them) are the imbibing and ingenuous hotel chambermaid Mary Lou (Candy Clark), who becomes his live-in caretaker, and the disillusioned, womanizing science professor Nathan Pryce (Rip Torn), who goes to work for him because he likes the fact that World Enterprises is "dumping computers and installing human beings...to bring back human errors because that's the way you get to new ideas." But guzzling gin and having a cocoon of money can make you aimless. Water all around you can make you lose touch with your identity and past. Like Icarus, you fall from grace. You become a little lost, a little damned.

Roeg was already familiar with the vagaries of beautifully damned superstars from directing Mick Jagger in his first film, *Performance* (1970). But when he arrived at chez Bowie for his meeting, only Angela (Mrs. Bowie) was there to greet him. After eight hours of waiting in the kitchen, his host returned. Feeling that Roeg and Paul Mayersberg's script was just another knockoff of Robert Heinlein's novel *Stranger in a Strange Land*, Bowie flat asked Roeg, "It's a bit corny, isn't it?" Bowie remembers, "His face just fucking fell off. Then he started talking. Two or three hours later I was convinced he was a genius."

Mayersberg boasted that the director aimed to make "a time machine of a movie." And as Roeg reported, "I wanted to take away the reliance on the literary form. But when you take that crutch away it rather upsets people. I also thought I'd like to play with the one thing in life to which we're absolute slaves—and that's time....It was the closest I could get to an extraordinary science fiction feel more than a look." Thanks to the exquisite eye of cinematographer Tony Richmond, countless rewrites, and a fine cast willing to learn day by day what they'd be shooting next in the beautiful wilds of

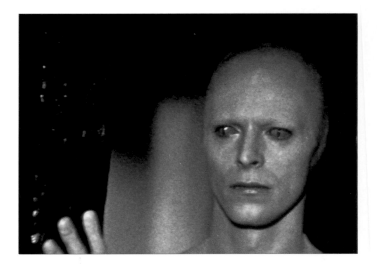

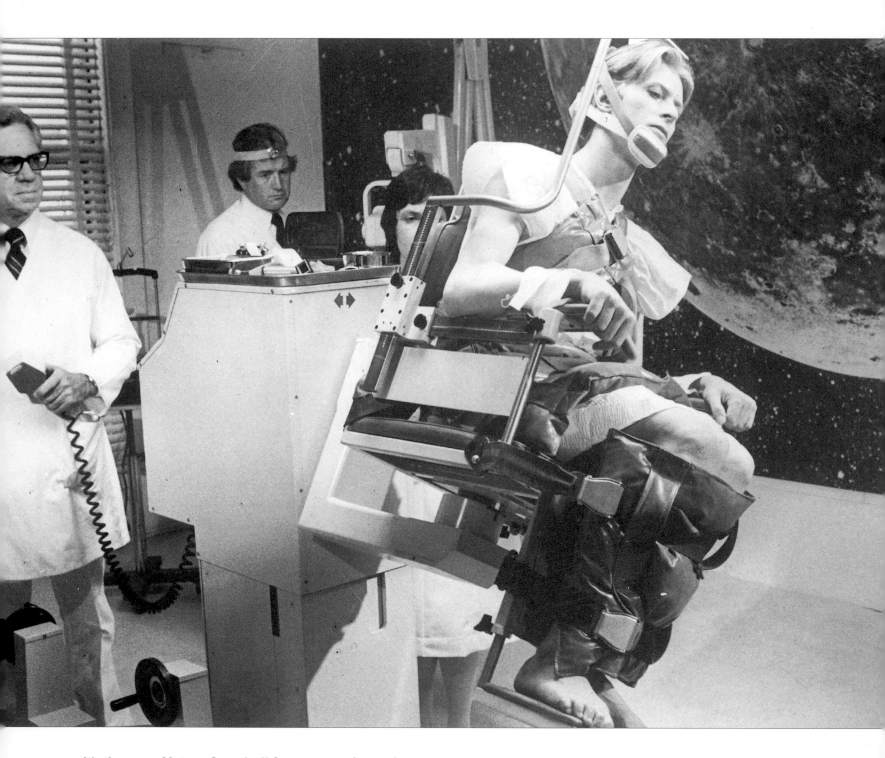

It's the same old story. Once the U.S. government learns that it has a real alien in its midst, it likes to experiment on him, not deport him.

New Mexico, this moody mosaic of a film melds from Earth to Newton's desert planet, and from Kabuki combat to a mind-meld with Pryce during his own ferocious foreplay with one of his coeds. Grief flows between paranoia and elation, which are flanked by danger and tenderness, almost slipping between realities.

Bowie, who unabashedly admitted, "I couldn't have worked with someone I considered to be less than myself—and I have a very, very high opinion of my own abilities," did not overestimate himself, either. Spending his off-camera time working on numerology, putting very visible ice-cream pounds onto his ultraslim frame, and almost dying from a bizarre case of milk poisoning, he

seems a seasoned screen actor. Mayersberg was amazed at his grasp of continuity, catching a fumbled drink the same way take after take. Clark was astounded by his professional willingness to continually run lines. Roeg was amazed at his ability to listen, at his uncanny instincts in front of a camera, and that he was easily dissuaded from providing the background music (so sweetly and spookily composed by John Phillips). Maybe he is an alien, because movie stars don't act like that.

At journey's end *The Man Who Fell to Earth* seems to span both Newton's whole lifetime and a flickering instant. Roeg acknowledged that "it has people puzzled whether twenty-five minutes or twenty-five years have passed in the film." This meant that the film was too long for the American distributor, which lopped off twenty-two minutes (after consulting a screenwriter, editor, a psychiatrist, and a whole group of Dartmouth students) from the British Lion film for the American release.

Out went some of the more graphic lovemaking scenes (a specialty of Roeg's) between Newton and Mary Lou, including one involving a blank-shooting pistol. Gone, as well, was Mary Lou's all-too-human reaction (peeing down her leg) to the climactic revelation of her lover's true appearance. Luckily for us, in 1997 a director's cut is available on laser disc and videotape. So sit down and get the feeling of what it means to be a million miles from home, even if the plotting sequencing seems to be not of this earth. You may be witnessing a new cinematic form. And as film critic Stephen Farber so aptly said, "If *The Man Who Fell to Earth* is ultimately disappointing, it fails on a level that most filmmakers will never even approach."

HOME IS WHERE THE HEART IS

When Steven Spielberg was on location in the Far East shooting *Raiders of the Lost Ark* (1981), he was feeling a little lonely. In a habit born of childhood (a childhood with divorced parents), each night alone in his tent he dreamed up an imaginary alien friend to keep him company. He imagined a gentle being who had been left behind during an expedition to gather botanicals when large, noisy men with official keys dangling from their belts gave chase to the sighted UFO. The lonelier Spielberg got the more he wanted to make a movie about this visitor, a paean to what he in his suburban youth had always wished to see.

Harrison Ford's wife, Melissa Mathison, who had coscripted *The Black Stallion* (1979) with J.G. Ballard, knew something about innocence, and since developing writer's block she had been hanging around the set of her hubby's film. When Spielberg pitched the idea of "the little guy who gets left behind" to her, she originally said no. However, the more she thought about it, the better it sounded. One day when she and Spielberg were turning over rocks and looking for scorpions together, she said yes.

For eight weeks the two met stateside to talk about this story about a ten-year-old suburban kid named Elliott, very similar to Spielberg, who finds someone—or something—rooting around in his absent dad's backyard shop. He runs into the creature in the nearby woods (where they both scream and run away, the creature

With a face only a mother could love—that ambassador of interplanetary understanding, E.T., is giving earthling Henry Thomas the finger (in the nicest possible way).

This extraterrestrial is looking pretty terrestrial—all that's missing is Monday night football.

squeaking like a helpless little critter). Finally, after drawing it out with a trail of Reeses Pieces (M & M's didn't want to do the publicity drive for the movie, so the newcomer candy got to triple its sales), Elliott discovers that he's hosting a three-foot-six-inch (107cm) tall, overly curious, slightly befuddled, very homesick, very loving extraterrestrial.

While the director was supervising the editing of *Raiders of the Lost Ark* (1981), Mathison went through three drafts (in which, among other changes, Elliott's Eddie Haskellesque best friend was deleted; the kids-versus-the-E.T.-chasing-adults confrontation was built up; and Spielberg's own touch, E.T. getting into the beer in the fridge, was gloriously added). Suffice it to say that the result was the most popular film of all time (until Spielberg's *Jurassic Park*, 1993).

Spielberg had storyboarded every inch of fantasy films like *Raiders*, but didn't want to "pencil" himself into a corner—not when he was going to be working almost exclusively with kids. He auditioned hundreds. Dee Wallace would play the beleaguered single mom. Then innocent Drew Barrymore would be the pesky little sister, who Elliott catches dressing his visitor up in doll clothes. Robert MacNaughton would be Elliott's exasperated, preteen older brother, whose bicycling cronies would be E.T.'s last best hope of getting home. Then he interviewed a San Antonio boy named Henry Thomas who gave a lousy, nervous reading but whose improv was so totally Elliott that Spielberg told him, with the camera still running, "You've got the job, kid."

Then there was E.T. to deal with. After wasting $700,000 (that's right) on a prototype that was scrapped, Spielberg hired Italian sculptor and model maker Carlo Rambaldi (who had already done exquisite work in the remake of *King Kong*, 1976, and made believable aliens in *Close Encounters of the Third Kind*) to give him a creature with a look that was both youthful and aged, a being with eyes like Albert Einstein and a rump like Donald Duck, something unsure of its footing. As Spielberg said, "He's much more conditioned to a heavier atmosphere, a heavier gravity. He's a little clumsy on Earth, always stumbling, getting knocked into by refrigerators, hitting walls." With a four-member crew working fifteen to twenty hours a day for six months, Rambaldi had produced three E.T.s, each model made of an aluminum-and-steel skeleton covered in fiberglass, polyurethane, and foam rubber. The price tag for all three was $1.5 million.

For medium shots, one E.T. was mechanically operated by a crew of a dozen people with cables to perform 150 individual movements. For close-ups, an electronic E.T. had airbladders on his head and chest to simulate breathing and facial expressions. For walking there was an E.T. suit that would admit a dwarf operator. As for that raspy, squeaky E.T. voice, though Debra Winger originally lent her efforts, some of which were used, when Ben Brutt, George Lucas' Skywalker Sound's sound designer, heard two-packs-of-cigarettes-a-day Pat Welsh, a retired elocution teacher, talking at the counter of a camera store, he knew he had hit pay dirt. Pat got a princely $380 to spend nine hours speaking about phoning home and other things in the recording studio.

There were other serendipitous moments. Hacking around, Henry Thomas generously offered E.T. a Coke. Spielberg loved the

Americana. And speaking of caffeine, when mime Caprice Rothe, who was over-javaed, got the shakes while maneuvering E.T.'s hands for his raid on the family fridge, her director loved the tremulous grab for all those new goodies. When Spielberg said, "I wanted a creature that only a mother could love," he couldn't have expected that 200 million surrogate mothers would be watching.

What a movie! *E.T. The Extra-Terrestrial* (1982) is science at its best (kid and alien ingenuity save the day) and its most threatening (SWAT teams of nasty scientists ready to make E.T. a lab specimen). Miracles performed, a spaceship (designed by Ralph McQuarrie) practically out of Jules Verne. Who could forget how adorable E.T. looked trick-or-treating, or hiding in a toy closet, or nurturing a flower with his glowing finger?

After two days' shooting in Culver City, California, eleven in Tujunga and Northridge (the epicenter of the 1993 L.A. earthquake), forty-two in the studio replicating the upper and lower floors of Elliott's home and the surrounding redwood forest, and six days on the Oregon border doing deep-woods work, Spielberg was in ahead of schedule if not under budget. Then it was on to postproduction to make (among other things) one of the best bike rides ever.

With E.T.'s empathic powers to feel human pain and to relieve it, his final bond with his Earth savior and friend (each saving each other's lives at crucial moments) is impossible to watch dry-eyed unless you club baby seals in your spare time. As Spielberg says, "This movie is really about fatherhood. The three kids have been abandoned by their father—and what do they find? Someone who knows what they're thinking and feeling, who can heal them when they've been hurt and make them laugh. E.T. is the father that we all wish we'd had or would like to be." This alien really did come in peace.

THEY'RE BACK

They're back. Nasty, slimy, lethal, world-domineering, colonizing, cold, reptilian, insectoid, government-conspiring, teeth-flashing, claw-catching, body-snatching aliens were back and they meant business—that is, show business. The self-involved me-generation of the seventies gave way to the what-the-hell-happened-to-my-future generation of the eighties. As political upheaval rocked Iran, Britains hunkered down to life under Margaret Thatcher, Nicaraguans adapted to a Marxist regime, South Korea's president was accidentally shot dead by his chief of intelligence, the Soviet Army invaded Afghanistan, and a little place called Three Mile Island narrowly averted Meltdown U.S.A., director Ridley Scott kicked us into the next two decades of extraterrestrial unrest with *Alien* (1979).

E.T. and *Close Encounters* designer Carlo Rambaldi along with Michael Seymour and Roger Dickens outdid themselves in providing the ever-mutating and -mutilating creature who sneaks aboard a vast mining-ore ship ten months from Earth. Swiss surre-

alist illustrator H.R. Giger provided the sinister, skeletal, prehistoric yet futuristic sets for it to live in. Science fiction's first kickass heroine, Ripley (Sigourney Weaver), provided some toe-to-toe combat for the jaws inside dripping jaws inside dripping jaws. And director Scott provided enough blood-soaked terror to give many a viewer both a heart attack and a queasy stomach simultaneously.

With Freddie Kreuger, Jason, and Michael Meyers dominating the human monster scene, horror took hold of sci-fi's traditional domain of monsters arriving on Earth, more often than not mixing in some laughs with the gore. There were toothy, hungry little *Critters* (1986) and their sequential progeny. There was the infectious *Night of the Creeps* (1986). Tongue was planted firmly in cheek when aliens came to Earth to harvest the latest galactic fad in fast food, human flesh, in the appropriately named yet hilarious *Bad Taste* (1988). Who had the courage to laugh at *Killer Klowns from Outer Space* (1988)?

ABOVE: More goo for your box-office dollar. The 1988 remake of The Blob *was just a tad more graphic than the 1958 original with Steve McQueen. OPPOSITE: We can see why Ripley (Sigourney Weaver) looks so grim, as she faces off with the most horrific creature to ever stalk a space crew in the nerve-shattering* Alien.

There was a bevy of both better and worse remakes like John Carpenter's Antarctic nightmare *The Thing* (1982), the Traci Lords camp sexploitation of the Roger Corman classic *Not of this Earth* (1988), the excellent remake of *The Blob* (1988), the militaristically set *Body Snatchers* (1994), and John Carpenter's star-studded remake of *Village of the Damned* (1995). Aliens even learned to say the right words to make us relax while they killed us in *I Come in Peace* (1990).

The midnineties have seen special effects rule on an extraterrestrial extravaganza of alien-invasion movies. The space-shoot-'em-up *Stargate* (1994) took soldier (Kurt Russell) and Egyptologist (James Spader) alike through a porthole in a pyramid to the other side of the universe to meet the sun god Ra (Jaye Davidson). The result of alien DNA injected into a human ovum was a lovely yet lethal, age-accelerated progeny let loose in the fleshpots of L.A. with the task of finding (and later killing) a disease-free sperm donor to help her hypergestate and further her *Species* (1995).

The Arrival (1996) pitted a lone radio astronomer (Charlie Sheen) against an insidious, alien plot to "terraform" the earth for mass colonization after accelerating global warming through the release of huge amounts of greenhouse gases from high-tech power stations scattered throughout the Third World. The loathsome creatures are crazy enough looking to hide back-bending knee joints, floppy brain flaps, and guttural clicking speech under

incredible makeup and are sane enough to say, "If you can't take care of your planet then you don't deserve to live here," as arch-villain Ron Silver does. Tim Burton's *Mars Attacks* (1996), though delayed when his famous stop-motion and modeling didn't impress producers, amused, amazed, and even horrified with a vengeance thanks to a revised live-action format and all-star cast. None other than Jack Nicholson played the president of the United States (God help us!). But *Stargate* creators Roland Emmerich and Dean Devlin made sure aliens didn't have to plot anything insidious or hokey when they made the invading spaceships look fifteen miles (24km) long in what Devlin called "the largest model shoot ever attempted," the blow-'em-up summer blockbuster *Independence Day* (1996).

Emmerich, who made a forty-story-tall, forty-story-deep prison of the future for *Moon 44* (1990) with only $3,000, does wonders with *Independence Day*'s substantially bigger budget. One would never know it, but courtesy of *Batman Forever*'s (1995) Mike Joyce, the sets are scale models. There are up to eighteen-foot (5.5m) tall models of everything from Huey helicopters, F-18 fighters, and the president's plane to the Statue of Liberty, the Empire State Building, and, yes, the White House. In fact, the building at 1600 Pennsylvania Avenue destroyed by pyrotechnicians Volker Engel and Joe Viskocil is only twenty feet wide by eight feet tall (2.5 by 6m).

In scenes where the invaders take out Los Angeles (they obliterate New York City and Washington, D.C., as well) the duo's "Wall of Destruction" was used. First positioning an eight-by-twenty-foot (2.5 by 6m) city street scene of exacting models on a vertical base with a high-speed camera shooting from the ceiling, the pyrotechs meticulously released a fireball from below which rolled up (but seemingly rolled across) the length of the street. Next, extras running for their lives against a blue screen were matted onto the street with digitized explosions matted at specific points over their heads. The chaos was completed by footage of stunt drivers crashing cars on a real street being mixed into the edit.

Pretty neat stuff for the end of the world. With four hundred special effects sequences, each with up to ten elements often requiring shots all their

I'll take Manhattan, the Bronx, and Staten Island, too. No quarter for humanity as one of the super-sized invasion ships gets ready to rumble in **Independence Day** *(1996).*

own, it's no wonder this baby had a price tag of $70 million. But what would Howard Hawks have thought? If screen alien invasions get much more sophisticated or expensive it might be wise to invest matching funds in some kind of planetary defense fund.

WHAT'S YOUR E.T. IQ?

Over the past half-century, science fiction movies have given us a lot of visitors (especially in the fifties and eighties). See if you can connect the films to some of our more famous guests.

VISITOR

1. *This new-age fashion model is really here to lethally collect chemicals created by human sex.*
2. *These ancient space-vampires come in on a comet and vant to drink your soul.*
3. *You don't want to cheat on your wife when an alien has given her a big head.*
4. *This alien is headed for the hood.*
5. *You don't want to let this future cop drink sour milk on duty.*
6. *Only Jerry Lewis could come from Kreton.*
7. *If it could have spoken it might have said, "In space, no one can hear you scream."*
8. *I say, what bad luck to have your whole country turned into a toaster oven.*
9. *Some say* Alien *(1979) borrowed a bunch from this old clunker.*
10. *This invisible, seven-foot-two-inch (218cm) creature came to Earth for a little sport named Arnold.*
11. *Ray Harryhausen's Venusian on vacation in Rome finally gets conquered by the Coliseum.*
12. *Og and Zog battle Larry, Moe, and Curly Joe.*
13. *You can only see these thought controllers with the right specs.*
14. *Look behind his Foster Grants and you might see an alien looking for blood donors.*
15. *He looks an awful lot like her dead husband.*
16. *All he needs is an Earth female to bear his child.*
17. *This time it's the she-alien looking for a little breeding material.*
18. *Bela Lugosi posthumously starred in this celebrated, all-time turkey.*
19. *Forget* Twin Peaks*! This time he's only pretending to be FBI while he tracks a space killer.*
20. *These guys have alcohol for blood and like to molest teens on lovers' lane.*
21. *Coscripted by Lenny Bruce, this alien's ray gun has the horrible power to make people tell the truth.*
22. *These Florida oldsters have found more than the Fountain of Youth.*
23. *They come from the planet Remulac. Get the point?*
24. *Beneath his multicolored fur he's just another space-wolf.*
25. *If Charlton Heston visited them, it's only fair that they visit us.*
26. *This robot really grows on you but he's such an energy drain.*

VEHICLE

A: Liquid Sky *(1983)*
B: Escape from Planet of the Apes *(1971)*
C: Alien *(1979)*
D: Devil Girl from Mars *(1954)*
E: Not of This Earth *(1957)*
F: Lifeforce *(1985)*
G: Island of the Burning Doomed *(1967)*
H: The Rocket Man *(1954)*
I: Starman *(1984)*
J: Alien Nation *(1988)*
K: Earth Girls Are Easy *(1989)*
L: Attack of the 50 Ft. Woman *(1958)*
M: I Married a Monster from Outer Space *(1958)*
N: Cocoon *(1985)*
O: It! The Terror from Beyond Space *(1958)*
P: Invasion of the Saucer Men *(1957)*
Q: The Brother from Another Planet *(1984)*
R: Predator *(1987)*
S: They Live *(1988)*
T: Coneheads *(1993)*
U: 20 Million Miles to Earth *(1957)*
V: Visit to a Small Planet *(1960)*
W: Plan 9 from Outer Space *(1959)*
X: The Hidden *(1987)*
Y: The Three Stooges in Orbit *(1962)*
Z: Kronos *(1957)*

Answers

1=A, 2=F, 3=L, 4=Q, 5=J, 6=V, 7=C, 8=G, 9=O, 10=R, 11=U, 12=Y, 13=S, 14=E, 15=I, 16=M, 17=D, 18=W, 19=X, 20=P, 21=H, 22=N, 23=T, 24=K, 25=B, 26=Z

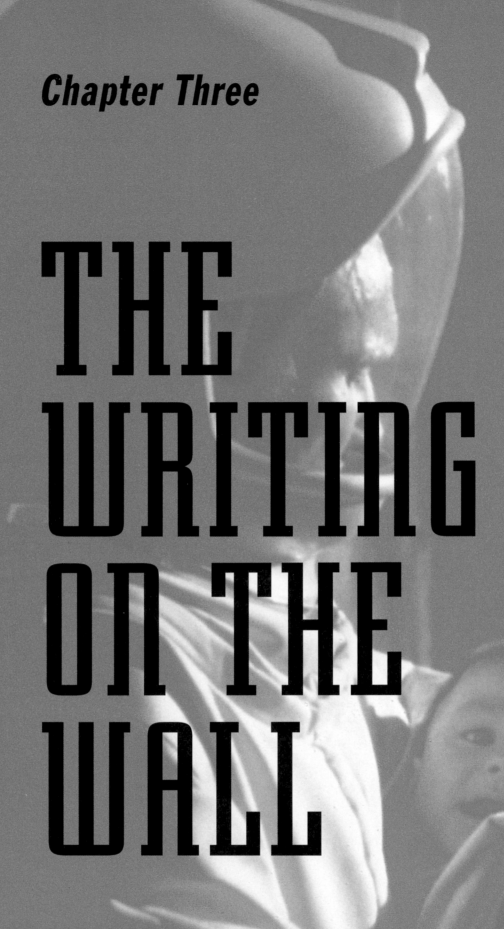

Chapter Three

THE WRITING ON THE WALL

The science fiction film probably offers more opportunities for messages, for themes, for comments, for talking about our society now or about where it's going, more than any other type of film.

—director Robert Wise

These soldiers are wondering how this baby was able to survive the space plague that wiped out an entire desert town and now threatens to infect Earth's entire population in the chillingly realistic clinical thriller **The Andromeda Strain.**

If some ancient prophets are correct, then the world (as we know it) should be ending sometime around two years after the publication of this book. If that's the case, then the warnings you are about to receive are pretty superfluous. On the other hand, if the prophets are wrong but the prognostications in the following films are right, it might be better if you had perished.

Apocalyptic literature has been around since man had sense enough to worry. The Bible's Book of Daniel predicted that the world would end by 160 B.C. Sixteenth-century France's plague physician and celebrated mystic, Nostradamus, supposedly forecasted calamity of every kind from the Great Fire of London to Napoleon's and Hitler's rises to the French Revolution, World War II, and the atom bomb in his cryptically written 1555 work, *The Centuries*. In modern times, naysayers from *Silent Spring*'s ecoconscious Rachel Carson to sociologist Alvin Toffler, the author of *Future Shock*, and gurus as diverse as Marshall McLuhan and Dwight Eisenhower have tried to warn us of the monsters society might spawn.

Need we remind ourselves that humanity's two million years on top of the food chain has been infinitesimal compared with the dinosaur's 165-million-year reign? And look what happened to them. Even some of the human populations on this planet have come and gone. The Anasazi disappeared without a trace. The Maya mysteriously withered away from their great city-states. Time and again we have overgrazed, overhunted, overfished, polluted, and deforested, not to mention battled ourselves into virtual oblivion.

Without recorded history, older civilizations can claim they didn't know better. They had no Holocaust film clips to watch, no ways to test ozone levels, no lists of endangered species, no equations of dwindling rain forest and CO_2 level in the atmosphere, no knowledge of a greenhouse effect. Today we know and we don't feel too great about it—not that it's made us change our wicked ways.

With the AIDS epidemic worldwide and ethnic cleansing abroad as well as race riots, rampant drug abuse, teen violence, militia standoffs, terrorist bombings, government conspiracies, oil spills, suicide doctors, Social Security depletion, genetic engineering, favored nation dictatorships, nuclear arsenals, organ thieves, and many other more fearsome facets of our existence, films of future annihilation or dystopia may seem a little beside the point. The future is now and we already know that we probably have the slave-master relationship between technology and man backward. Still, en route to the nihilistic, in the nervous nineties there have been some artistic voices to warn us of where we were going.

THE WORRIERS

And man said "What if...?" In the beginning there was the problem we could do nothing about. The earth could be destroyed. Comets were not just for watching through your telescope back at the turn of the century. French astronomer Camille Flammarion's 1894 novel *Le Fin du Monde* depicted a giant comet colliding with the earth sometime in the twenty-fifth century. Though in his book humanity survives, technology is refined, wars are ended, and psychic abilities are honed so earthlings can communicate with Mars and Venus, the rug is pulled by the final pages when a cooling at the planet's core soaks up all surface moisture, leaving us all to die of cold and thirst.

Since ancient times comets had been seen as harbingers of disaster. Some scientists say that such a rock from the sky at the end of the Cretaceous period sent up the dust that thickened the atmosphere that cooled the globe that brought on the Ice Age that killed the dinosaurs. More recently, on June 30, 1908, along Siberia's Tunguska River, a comet leveled thousands of acres with the force of a hydrogen bomb. The coming of Halley's comet in 1910 was thought by many to be the final curtain (though today we know that comet has passed the globe twenty times since 239 B.C. The 1910 silent film *The Comet* put this fear on film, showing mankind scrambling underground to find "uncontaminated" water. Since then cataclysmic cosmic collisions have been a favorite of filmmakers from George Pal's *When Worlds Collide* (1951) to the story of asteroids from a sun eruption, *The Day the Sky Exploded* (1958), to Tokyo's effort at using hydrogen gas jets to push Earth away from the magnetic meteor *Gorath* (1963) to the star-studded flop *Meteor* (1979).

OUT OF THE LABYRINTH

Barring obliteration by natural forces, there was still a wide variety of ways for humanity to make itself miserable if not dead. Technology combined with man's baser instincts was at the bottom of most of it. What if the future wasn't like a heroic Flash Gordon serial? What if the combined political and corporate states were so vast that they controlled every minute of most of humanity's waking and sleeping life? What if technology was so entrenched that men and women were just drones doing endlessly repetitive high-tech tasks, under enforced sedation from birth with their every bodily function monitored to nip unrest in the bud, so

neutered that they were hardly recognizable from one another, so soulless that they didn't even have the initiative to get out of a broken elevator? What if the only things that this zombified population could turn to for solace were a police force of brutal robots, a church of automated confessionals, and television that buried whatever instincts they had left with broadcasts of the most barren sex and violence imaginable?

Imagining it? Now insert protagonists into the scenario whose heroism consists of ditching their medication long enough to wake up to what's happened to them. Welcome to the twenty-fifth century and the little piece of future hell that George Lucas dreamed up while he was a film student at the University of Southern California—perhaps the grimmest, most all-encompassing, and most alienating look at the future ever filmed, *THX-1138* (1971).

THX-1138:4EB, whose treatment had been codeveloped with fellow USC student Walter Murch, was shot in ten days under the auspices of a cinematography class that Lucas was teaching. An

Welcome to the future—a white, sterile wasteland of humans reduced to drugged insects is what you'll find waiting for you in George Lucas' **THX 1138** *(1971).*

unflashy soundtrack of garbled audio broadcasts (thanks to sound specialist Murch) and dehumanizing computer graphics running across the bottom of the screen increased its realism. It won Lucas a scholarship with Columbia Pictures where he was set to work on the western *Mackenna's Gold* (1969).

When Coppola started his own independent operation, Zoetrope Studios, to bring new blood into Warner Bros. distribution, Lucas was his first choice to go with him and a full-budgeted remake of *THX-1138:4EB*, now simply titled *THX-1138*, was the first project he wanted Zoetrope to produce. Though at first Warner Bros. balked at the project, deal maker Coppola wooed them with a low budget ($777,777.77—guess his lucky number) and an inflated promise to do a script that Lucas had told him about, a Vietnam sto-

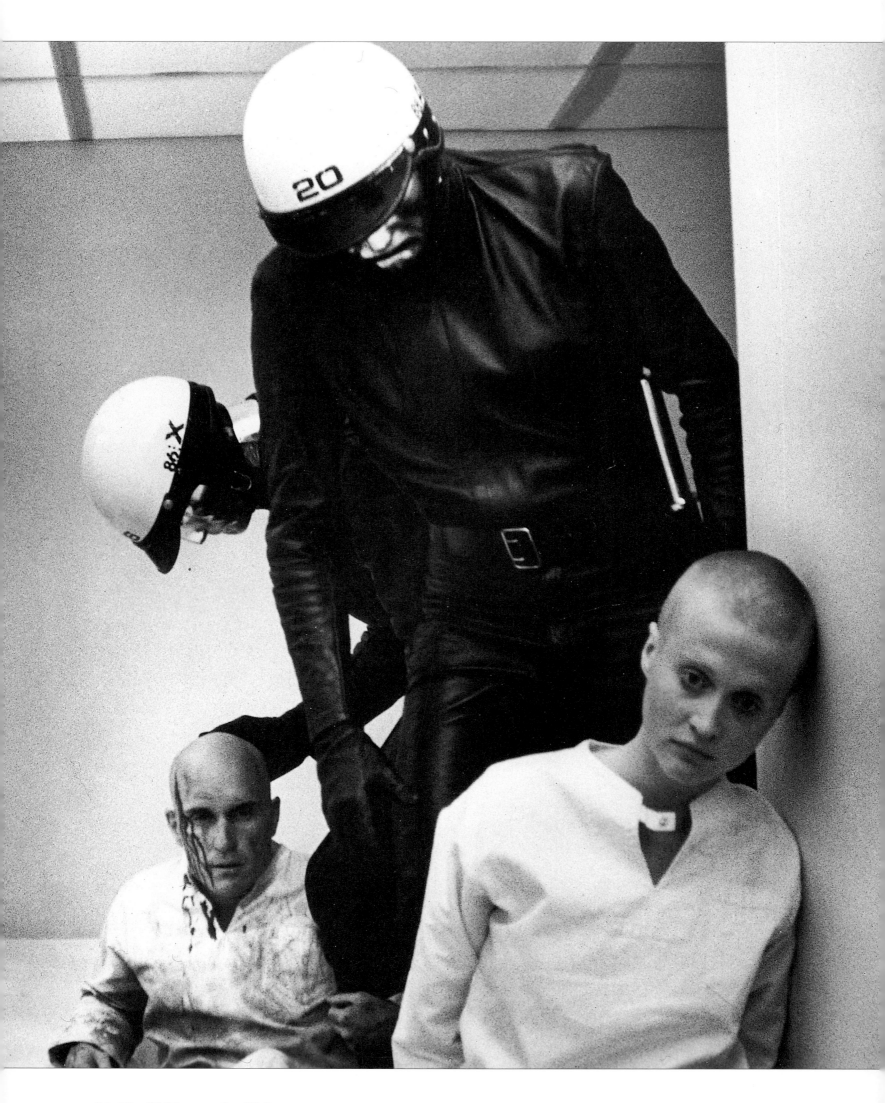

ry Lucas and classmate John Millius had kicked around at USC—a little thing called *Apocalypse Now* (1979).

Even at a meager salary of $15,000 (with an additional $25,000 promised for *Appocalypse Now*) Lucas jumped at the chance to fully realize his film. He felt, "I might never get the chance again to make this totally off-the-wall movie, without any real supervision. Once I did this, I thought they would never let me in the film business again." He set his shoot schedule for ten weeks, declined to put unaffordable initiation dues down with the Directors' Guild in case his worries turned out to be true, and went to work.

Coppola thought that all directors should write and set the twenty-three-year-old Lucas to expand the story into a feature script. The result was weak so Coppola hunkered down to help out, only driving the story away from Lucas' original conception. Scripter Oliver Hailey was hired on, but further diluted the director's vision. Only when Walter Murch came down from San Francisco to edit the sound for Coppola's *The Rain People* did the right words fly. As Murch said, "We just threw everything up into the air and watched it come down."

"Work hard, increase production, prevent accidents, and be happy." Those are words of techno-wisdom (announced by David Ogden Stiers, television's future Major Winchester of *M*A*S*H*) pumped again and again through the subterranean, sterile world that pale, bald-headed workers THX-1138 (Robert Duvall) and LUH-3417 (Maggie McOmie) inhabit. Coworkers and roommates in a white-on-white world, they handle radioactive isotopes by day. After mind-numbingly repeated activity, they retreat to a sedated, sexless, almost catatonic existence in their cramped cubicle at night.

As fate would have it LUH decides to stop taking her pills and, feeling the stirrings of emotions through the drug haze, gets THX to ditch his dose. Soon they are caring for each other and, yes, making love on the sly. Soon she is pregnant. Soon they need to be together. Soon he can't function through the formerly drug-eased repetition of excruciating work. Soon another worker with desires of his own, SEN-5241 (creepily played by Donald Pleasence), tries to sabotage their happiness. Soon all hell breaks loose.

Infractions can get a worker surrounded by a trio of towering, liquid metal-faced cops who leisurely electrocute with prod-batons. Dysfunction can get you exterminated or sent for a life in limbo at a fetterless prison of infinite white. It is from there that THX takes an even more terrifying chance, and with the help of a runaway hologram (yes, hologram) and a car capable of 235 miles

per hour (378kph), escape may be possible. But escape to what?

Lucas admitted that he "didn't want to alter things for the convenience of drama." This movie with its episodic format, documentary look, black-and-white video readouts, bare snippets of scenes, blurry images, "purposefully stupid music" of the future by Lalo Schiffrin, and mind-blowing meticulous marriage of sight and sound thanks to Murch's audio montages may be lean on plot but the chilling integrity of the vision is total. And despite the low budget, Lucas later claimed that it was the one movie he really enjoyed doing. As he would with *Star Wars* (1977), he built miniatures with model parts and a $10 fireworks assortment.

Equipment was hauled in trash cans. Techniscope was the camera of choice because it used less film, was easier to set up, and gave a wider look without fancy camera lenses. The van was borrowed from *The Rain People* set. Extras willing to shave their heads were scarce, so barber subjects were recruited from the Synanon drug rehab center. Futuristic interior sets in the San Francisco area included free use of the Marin County Civic Center (designed by Frank Lloyd Wright), the Oakland Colosseum, the Pacific Gas and Electric Building, the Lawrence Livermore Atomic Energy Lab, and the virgin tunnels of the yet-to-be-opened Bay Area Rapid Transit (BART) system.

It all makes an amazingly real world for $750,000—a world so alien that watching *THX-1138* is almost like watching a foreign film. Yet the horror has appallingly familiar moments. The most disturbing scene includes a background soundscape of laconic technicians discussing a problem while video footage of THX's contorting, twitching, helpless body on the floor plays. After a while you realize what...or who...the problem is. Similarly, the end of a labyrinthine chase is brought about not by defeat, but for an ironic reason that most film producers understand all too well.

Warner Bros. didn't understand and freaked at the final cut of Lucas' uncompromising picture, helping to bring about the demise of Zoetrope and using their own editor (Lucas had masterfully cut the original) to lop a meaningless four minutes from the white prison sequence. The public understood a little better, especially when *THX-1138* was rereleased after Lucas' rise to superstardom with *Star Wars*. Lucas' message, which goes so well with the film's final image, hits home: "We are living in cages with the door open."

SCIENCE FACTION

What if the plague days aren't over? What if a microbe really can wipe us out? In the sixth century, bubonic plague, spread by fleas who had fed on the blood of infected rats, killed 100 million people in Europe, Asia, and the Middle East. In the fourteenth century, pneumonic plague, contracted from breathing saliva particles spewed by infected persons, joined forces with bubonic in the Black Death that wiped out half of Europe's population by swelling their lymph nodes to the size of baseballs and filling their bodies with pus and their lungs with fluid.

"A tranquility so casual and thoughtless seemed almost effortlessly to give the lie to those old pictures of the plague: Athens, a charnel-house reeking to heaven and deserted even by the birds; Chinese towns cluttered up with victims silent in their agony; the convicts at Marseille piling corpses into pits; the building of the Great Wall in Provence to fend off the furious plague-wind; the damp, putrefying pallets stuck to the mud floor at the Constantinople lazar-house, where the patients were hauled up from their beds by hooks; the carnival of masked doctors at the Black Death; men and women copulating in the cemeteries of Milan; cartloads of dead bodies rumbling through London's ghoul-haunted darkness—nights and days filled always, everywhere, with the eternal cry of human pain."

—from *The Plague*, by Albert Camus (translation by Stuart Gilbert)

As recently as 1919, a pandemic of influenza killed off 22 million people worldwide before flu shots shut it down. Since then we've had polio, smallpox, and tuberculosis to contend with. More contemporarily, in 1976 researchers identified the Hanta virus, named for a river in Korea where the virus has been known for one thousand years. The disease, with its lung- and kidney-destroying hemorrhagic fever, is contracted from inhaling particles of rat or mouse feces and has recently run amok in the Four Corners area of the American Southwest. In 1979 and again in 1995 a highly contagious fever spawned from the banks of Zaire's Ebola River wiped out whole settlements in Africa, as we've seen dramatized in films like *Outbreak* (1995) and *Hot Zone* (1995). Pneumonic plague still kills thousands in India. And AIDS is a worldwide epidemic that has taken more than 295,000 lives (as of mid-1995) in the United States alone.

Those are the natural killers. Now to the ones we manufacture for war. During the Indian Wars of the 1800s the U.S. Army set a grisly precedent by giving gifts of cholera- and smallpox-germ-infested blankets to immunologically unprepared Indians, thus adding a little biological kick to the rest of their genocide. Luckily, since then governments have usually opted for chemical weapons like lung-destroying mustard gas, which was used in WWI. While Japan allegedly used Soviet and Chinese prisoners for bacteriological experiments in the late thirties, countless other countries also made biological deterrents, using animals as their guinea pigs.

Despite the long-standing 1925 Geneva Protocol, which banned the use of biologic weapons, the United States continued to develop death-dealing delights ready for deployment, such as staphylococcal food poisoning, Venezuelan equine encephalomyelitis, tularemia bacteria, and coccidioidomycosis fungus, not to mention animal-destroying foot-and-mouth disease and fowl-plague as well as crop-killing potato blight, stem rust, and rice blast.

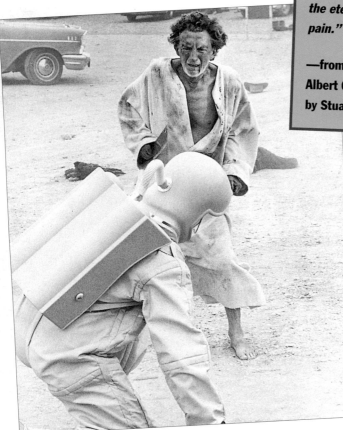

No sound of music here. Scientist James Olson must fend off one of the two survivors of a space plague in Robert Wise's sci-fi thriller The Andromeda Strain *(1970).*

The Vietnam War saw America's widespread use of defoliants like Agent Orange for wiping out the protective cover of the jungle's canopy with dioxin levels that gave thousands of American soldiers (let alone Vietnamese) cancer in the process. In 1979 an outbreak of anthrax poisoning in the then-U.S.S.R. was alleged to have occurred because of an accidental leak at a biological warfare factory. And while rumors have abounded that the water supplies of our enemies have been contaminated in covert CIA actions, that Gulf War syndrome was in part a result of exposure to biological weaponry, and that AIDS itself didn't begin with a monkey in the jungle but in a weapons lab, what is undeniable is that in 1990 the Department of Defense spent $600 million on research into this science fictionesque nightmare.

Michael Crichton brought the bad news home to science fiction. While still a Harvard med student in 1965, Crichton read an inspiring footnote in the textbook *The Major Features of Evolution*. It suggested that a writer should write some science fiction about organisms in the upper atmosphere. Crichton did and sold it to Hollywood while the book was still in galley form.

Crichton knew just how curious and paranoid the government and military were about what potential biological agents might be floating around in space. NASA's fear that Apollo moon astronauts might bring back some unstoppable contagion led NASA to keep them quarantined for weeks after their splashdowns. Crichton asked, "What if a satellite sent out into orbit also served the dual purpose of culling deep space for microbes that might be of use in germ warfare labs?"

In a dramatic and potentially suicidal moment, Olson removes his biohazard suit, much to George Mitchel and Paula Kelly's chagrin in **The Andromeda Strain.**

THIS IS THE WAY THE WORLD ENDS, NOT WITH A BANG BUT WITH CREDITS

Forrest Gump may have effused that "life is like a box of chocolates," but not everybody shares his optimism. See if these main characters help you match up the movie with the foul futures designed to fill them (and us) with dread and despair.

DESCRIPTION

1. Fun, games, and predators in a postnuclear ice age with Paul Newman.

2. Thought crime...Goldberg...Winston (John Hurt)...Julia (Suzanna Hamilton)..and Richard Burton as the elder sibling.

3. Welcome to the corporate killing ground and meet its undefeated rollerskating champ, Jonathan E (James Caan).

4. It's 2030 and being fertile in the Republic of Gilead (where a chemical accident left most women barren) can really make you (Natasha Richardson) a slave.

5. He (Bruno Lawrence) woke up one New Zealand morning to find everyone gone because of the energy grid he'd been working on.

6. Lee Majors, move over. In a world of sleazoid criminals and psychos, nobody messes with rebuilt authority figure Peter Weller.

7. This sub captain from down under (Gregory Peck) is waiting for the big atomic cloud to drift down so that he can sail off to see if home still exists.

8. Viva the twenty-first century Italian-style as killers (Ursula Andress and Marcello Mastroianni) are cultivated to channel aggression away from war and into the hunt.

9. Arnold Schwarzenegger knows that in entertainment-crazed 2019 Subzero will chill you, Buzzsaw will slash you, Dynamo will shock you, Fireball will fry you, and a nation will watch you with commercial breaks.

10. When he's not using "the scoop" to move some of his paralyzed city's sweltering, starving populace, cop Charlton Heston wonders just what exactly is feeding those 40 million hungry New Yorkers.

11. The crystal they planted in Michael York's hand at birth goes from red to yellow to green to black. By age thirty his time is up and mandatory extermination is put into play.

12. Don Johnson needs something smarter than himself to survive and meet chicks in the postnuke wasteland, but who really is his best friend?

13. Melanie Griffith can track into the gang-filled future to hunt down a replacement for the robotic mate her client got attached to.

14. Mel Gibson is up to his eyeballs in postapocalyptic pig-doo deep below the desert's Bartertown and on his way to 3-D combat with the Master Blaster (both giant and dwarf).

15. Julie Christie teaches fireman Oskar Werner the beauty of memorizing Poe.

16. Lawrence Pressman says the bugs are taking over. Just watch 'em!

17. The serum from his nonvampiric blood makes Charlton Heston humanity's last best hope.

18. Hit-and-run driving is no longer a felony but a national sport for the likes of David Carradine.

19. If Rock Hudson doesn't feel quite like himself, it may

LEFT: Microchip-implanted courier, Keanu Reeves gets ready to do some drastic downloading. Surfing the net has never been more "mind blowing" than in *Johnny Mnemonic* (1995).

DYSTOPIA

A: **Logan's Run** *(1976)*

B: **The Omega Man** *(1971)*

C: **The Handmaid's Tale** *(1990)*

D: **Escape from L.A.** *(1996)*

E: **Nineteen Eighty-Four** *(1984)*

F: **A Boy and His Dog** *(1975)*

G: **The Quiet Earth** *(1985)*

H: **Seconds** *(1966)*

I: **Mad Max Beyond Thunderdome** *(1985)*

J: **Soylent Green** *(1973)*

K: **Quintet** *(1979)*

L: **The Tenth Victim** *(1965)*

M: **Cherry 2000** *(1988)*

N: **Death Race 2000** *(1975)*

O: **Rollerball** *(1975)*

P: **Blade Runner** *(1982)*

Q: **RoboCop** *(1987)*

R: **Fahrenheit 451** *(1967)*

S: **The Hellstrom Chronicle** *(1971)*

T: **On the Beach** *(1959)*

U: **The Stepford Wives** *(1975)*

V: **The Running Man** *(1987)*

W: **No Blade of Grass** *(1970)*

X: **Johnny Mnemonic** *(1995)*

Y: **Testament** *(1983)*

Z: **The Last Man on Earth** *(1964)*

be because he's the new and improved body that a tired, old executive has just slipped into...for a ghastly price.

20. Nigel Davenport knows what happens when a sinister smog kills every crop on Earth leaving England with a week's supply of food.

21. Flatfoot Harrison Ford is getting lessons in life and death in L.A. (Los Androids).

22. Katherine Ross is finding the mechanics of suburban living a little menacing.

23. What's a little missing childhood for Keanu Reeves when it leaves so much lovely storage space?

24. This time it's Vincent Price's turn to hold the fort against the bloodsuckers.

25. Jane Alexander doesn't have to worry about World War III. It's here, but not for long.

26. If Snake Plissken (Kurt Russell) can get the president off the island of Manhattan he can break in and out of this new edition.

OPPOSITE: Opposite worlds collide as Oskar Werner falls for Julie Christie and literature in *Fahrenheit 451.*

Answers

1=K, 2=E, 3=O, 4=C, 5=G, 6=Q, 7=T, 8=L, 9=V, 10=J, 11=A, 12=F, 13=M, 14=I, 15=R, 16=S, 17=B, 18=N, 19=H, 20=W, 21=P, 22=U, 23=X, 24=Z, 25=Y, 26=D

What makes this thriller so thrilling and yet so real? The Project Wildfire team: biologist Jeremy Stone, pathologist Charles Dutton, surgeon Mark Hall, and microbiologist Ruth Leavitt are no glamourpusses but believably beleaguered, middle-aged professionals at the end of their ropes, who are running out of time and are as often at each other's throats as they are in each other's corners. Leavitt was originally a man in Crichton's book. Then Gidding marched into Wise's office with a sex-change suggestion.

"Get the hell out of here with that kind of crazy idea," barked Wise. "I can just see the reviews now: 'There's Raquel Welch in the submarine again.'" Wise was referring to the terrible press that the sex symbol had received in *Fantastic Voyage* (1966). But Gidding's Leavitt was an out-of-shape woman in her forties, with an appetite for chain-smoking, an acid tongue, and a closet case of epilepsy. Kate Reid is superlative as the curmudgeonly microbe hunter, as are Arthur Hill as the lead biologist, David Wayne as the warm workhorse of a pathologist, and James Olson as the slightly rebellious surgeon in whose hands the fate of the planet finally rests.

Biologist Jeremy Stone (Arthur Hill), leader of Project Wildfire, is at his wits end and time is running out as a scientific safehaven becomes a literal time bomb in The Andromeda Strain.

Suppose it crashed in Piedmont, New Mexico. Suppose some dumb country doctor decided to open it up. Suppose the space plague inside it killed everybody for miles around in a matter of seconds (for the lucky ones) to minutes (for the unlucky), turning every drop of blood in their bodies into powder. Suppose it was up to the four doctors and scientists of the top-secret Project Wildfire to bring the deadly capsule back to a gargantuan underground lab so that they can analyze and exterminate the lethal cargo. Suppose their only clue was the two who miraculously survived the epidemic, an old sterno drinker and a near-newborn baby. Suppose they discovered the terrifying truth only to have things go very, very wrong—end-of-the-world wrong.

You won't see slimy aliens and cool spaceships when you watch Universal's *The Andromeda Strain* (1971), but you will be nailed to your seat with fear and suspense by a film so uncomfortably documentary in feel that you may run out and buy a biohazard suit when it's all over. From the moment the movie begins, with special effects, computer-fed superimpositions of classified documents, Xrays, and microphotography overlaying the credits and Gil Melle's alien, mechanized, nonmusical music, you know this is as far from sci-fi schlock as you can get. With director Robert Wise at the helm, a suspenseful screenplay by Nelson Gidding (which for once makes tech talk sound real), and *2001: A Space Odyssey* (1968) special effects meister Douglas Trumbull making magnificent use of his $550,000 chunk of a $6.5 million budget, this is a rare science fiction gem. It plays like horrifying fact.

The technical flash in this high-tech movie has a lot to do with equipment. From the original army-satellite pickup team's use of nightscopes to a jet pilot's aerial photography to the biohazard suits and limited oxygen that the Wildfire team has to go into town with, the gear and gadgets are awesomely real. The five-story, largely steel-and-glass $300,000 replica of NASA's lunar receiving lab was so immense (sixty-seven feet [20m] tall) that a one-floor excavation was dug under Universal's soundstage #12 to accommodate the film.

Inside this labyrinthine set (where the team has to undergo a sixteen-hour decontamination process that includes being subjected to long-wave radiation, getting a physical exam from a computer, being scanned for fungal lesions by a "body analyzer," getting pneumatic booster immunizations, and having xenon lamps burn away their outer layers of skin), $4 million worth of very real, very borrowed instrumentation was used from both Cal Tech and the Jet Propulsion Laboratory. It's fascinating stuff to watch in action.

Stone uses mechanical hands to handle the analysis of what turns out to be a lethal, constantly mutating, energy-consuming crystalline life-form. Hall examines his survivors not just through the glove box used in most lab incubators but an entire bodysuit reached through an accordioning plastic tunnel that enables him to move about an airtight exam room. Leavitt searches for the deadly particle in the metal mesh of the satellite with microphotography that seems to magnify to infinity. All this supertechnical realism created hurdles that inspired cast and crew to dub the picture "The Heavenly Hernia."

Much of what scientists and audiences view in the film (with cinematographer Richard H. Kline's cool split-screen photography) comes from closed-circuit TV screens. However, closed-circuit screens with their six hundred lines of resolution photographed so badly that twenty-eight-year-old Trumbull had to devise screens with more than three times the clarity. The gargantuan set had to be refrigerated (necessitating parkas for the cast) to 50°F (10°C) to make poison gas look like it billowed up five stories. But the smoke kept causing the real lasers (that in the film detect and destroy any escaped lab animals) to malfunction during Hall's climactic climb up a sixty-foot (18m) ladder through the compound's columnar core as he tries to avert disaster. The required camera angles for the climb made it impossible to put safety nets below actor Olson, who was deathly afraid of heights (that sweat on his brow is not heat-induced).

Perhaps the stickiest science wicket to get through was finding a way to make monkeys and a rat appear to actually die as the team uses finer and finer air filters to test the size of the organism. For this problem USC's Department of Veterinary Medicine suggested enclosing the animals in an airtight container over a three-foot (91.5cm) container of CO_2. The animals would seem to die but would only slowly lose consciousness before the cameras clicked off and pure oxygen was given to them.

All this technology would be overkill if the players and the screenplay didn't keep us breathless. Wise maintains incredible pressure and then kicks it into overdrive for the final hour of the film as the lab itself becomes a monster, threatening to annihilate the scientists who have become foreign bodies in a living, man-made organism. And if their imminent destruction isn't enough to chill, there's always the image of what will result—the sight of a scalpel slicing open a cadaver's wrist only to have blood sift out like desert sand.

THE GUARDING OF THE GREEN

What if technology wins out over ecology? What if the eco-freaks were right all along? What if Earth's forests (rain and otherwise) make way for a burgeoning humanity on a poisoned and over-populated planet? What if we're stripped down to one big strip-mall?

Douglas Trumbull has learned a little bit about technology in his long and illustrious career in science fiction films. Most recently, he pioneered the mind-blowing, crystal-clear, gargantuan

"Trees within the Connecticut Arboretum Natural Area were seriously injured when the town of Waterford sprayed the roadside with chemical weed-killers in 1957. Even large trees not directly sprayed were affected. The leaves of the oaks began to curl and turn brown, although it was the season for spring growth. Then new shoots began to put forth and grew with abnormal rapidity, giving a weeping appearance to the trees. Two seasons later, large branches on these trees had died, others were without leaves, and the deformed, weeping effect of whole trees persisted."

—from *Silent Spring*, by Rachel Carson

images possible with Showscan filming technology. Years earlier, he ditched Hollywood to create the greatest theme park attraction ever, Back to the Future: The Ride, at Univeral Studios. Before that, he helmed the chilling look at scientists recording and transmitting individuals' perceptions in *Brainstorm* (1983). He was the special effects legend behind such landmark films as *Blade Runner* (1982), *Star Trek—The Motion Picture* (1979), *Close Encounters of the Third Kind* (1977), and *The Andromeda Strain* (1971).

In 1971 Trumbull knew just how cool technology could be. Working with Stanley Kubrick for two and a half years on *2001: A Space Odyssey* (1968) had changed his life. He knew that machines were "simply the tools of man," though so often treated as somehow evil in themselves on film. For his directorial debut, he was looking for a story about a good man-machine relationship. Society's neglect of the environment and one man's inner demons would be the villians.

So began a small film cherished by film and ecology freaks alike, the cult classic *Silent Running* (1971). The date is 2071 and for ten years the crew of American Airlines' space-freighter Valley Forge have been shepherding an unusual cargo around the sun. Back on Earth, where the temperature is a uniform 75°F (24°C), there is no unemployment, no war, and no vegetation.

ABOVE: The biodomes of the space freighter Valley Forge house what few plants that humankind (if not Earth) still possesses in Silent Running. LEFT: Ecologist run amok, Bruce Dern gets some medical treatment from one of the only companions he has left, a droid named Dewey in Silent Running.

is only one human on board and no dialogue) are working stiffs who love their synthetic chow and their wild rides on the cavernous freighter's dune buggies but don't give a hoot about the ecosystems they're presumably escorting until Earth is stable enough to reintroduce them. None cares except one, a boyish-looking botanist with a zealot's gleam who sleeps with a conservation pledge tacked next to his bunk, wears monkish robes, delights in real food, swims nude, and hums Smokey the Bear songs when he's stressed.

The crew learns from command that Earth has given up on replanting the forests and other vegetation and wants the

What survives is present only in the complete ecosystems contained inside the huge, glass, geodesic domes carried by the Valley Forge.

This is the workaday world of space, and the men who inhabit it (although in Trumbull's original twelve-page treatment there

freightermen to nuke their botanical loads as their huge ship orbits around Jupiter. Most of the boys are buoyant about going home and celebrate by hot-rodding their dune buggies all over the ship and playing poker and billiards (on a circular table with a pocket in the center). Freeman Lowell (played by a young Bruce Dern), however, is freaking out at the prospect of returning to an earth he despises and destroying its last forests. In a fracas over their orders, the wounded Freeman kills one crewmate and then jettisons the other two to die with the biodome they're detonating. He's made his choice—ecolife over human. But what will happen to him from here?

This is what the movie peruses—a man alone, with an impossible mission and a burning conscience. Well, not exactly alone. Before R2D2 ever beeped and buzzed his way into our hearts, Trumbull's Huey, Dewey, and Louie (a.k.a. Drones 1, 2, and 3) made robots a beautiful thing. These squat little waddling creations are perhaps the true stars of this moving movie. Sentinels, gardeners, and companions, they do everything from perform surgery on Freeman's shattered leg to learn to bluff at poker (a hilarious scene) and manage to appear anxious as Freeman later operates on one of them who has been bashed when the ship is buffeted through one of Saturn's rings.

Amazingly, there were people in those three-foot (91.5cm) tall toddlers. Bilateral amputees Mark Pearsons, Steven Brown, Cheryl Sparks, and Larry Wisehunt make metal come to life at a substantially lower price than animatronics would have. But with no Kubrick here to foot the bill, necessity was the mother of invention on this $1.3 million film with a $300,000 tech budget. Trumbull got tons of material donated from industries including the polyurethane foam and vacuum-formed styrene plastic that made most of his sets. Those sets were set up not at a studio soundstage but, for a little more than $3,000 a month, in the interior of the retired aircraft carrier Valley Forge rusting in L.A. harbor. "We had permission to do anything we wanted to the carrier," Trumbull noted, "as long as we didn't remove any metal."

The seven-foot (2m) -high ceilings and fixed walls on the carrier may have been cramped, but space was no problem when creating the botanical forest inside an unused hangar at the small airport in Van Nuys, California. It's hard to imagine that a few tons of earth, some wading pools from Sears, and plants from a local nursery could look so convincing. Trumbull's inventiveness extends everywhere on the film. As he had in the "Dawn of Man" sequences for *2001* he uses front-screen projection (a glass-beaded surface bouncing a projected image back into a camera lens) to create the starscape outside the geodesic domes. Trumbull boasted that an unheard-of 95 percent of the special effect was caught on the original negative, leaving a postshoot optical bill of a scant $8,000.

Sometimes Trumbull's do-it-yourselfness had an added payback. Along with friend and onetime designer for Honda trail bikes and Hughes helicopters Hiroshi Kira, Trumbull came up with a nonpolluting all-terrain vehicle that quickly merited marketing interest. His unsatisfactory investigation of various prosthetic arms for his drones led him to invent a lightweight and inexpensive solution that was soon sought by the American Machine Foundry Company. No wonder Trumbull wanted to make a machine-friendly movie. He was on pretty palsy terms with them, or in his own words, "I have a point of view that doesn't look at them with fear."

Silent Running (originally a World War II term to describe running submarines with their engines low enough that enemies overhead cannot detect them), with its greenery, Joan Baez soundtrack, and infinite gentleness, was planned "to be the opposite of sophistication," according to its director. Yet as simple and gentle as its message was, the world that has brought Freeman to this crossroads is a chilling thought indeed. And the ultimate decision he faces (in which the drones play a heartbreaking part) is one of the toughest to grace a science fiction movie, big budget or small.

REAL HORRORSHOW, OR, "WHAT'S IT GOING TO BE THEN, EH?"

What if violence is only going to escalate as time progresses? Gangbangers on our streets. Metal detectors in our high school hallways. Pop music thrilling to cop killing. Kiddies in our courts charged for having savaged toddlers and infants (blaming movies like *Child's Play*, 1988, as their inspiration, no less). Some sociologists forecast a chilling future where younger and younger "superpredators" are the practitioners of more and more heinous crimes. The number of homicides committed by kids under seventeen years of age tripled from 1984 to 1994 and promises to grow by another 25 percent by 2005. Gee, if that old saw "There's no such thing as a bad boy" doesn't ring quite as true today, how will it sound tomorrow?

Enter Stanley Kubrick, a book by Anthony Burgess called *A Clockwork Orange*, and a teen protagonist named Alex who could cripple Huck Finn, David Copperfield, and Holden Caulfield with one hand tied behind his back. Burgess had been drawn to the book by his wife's rape by three GIs during London's bombing blackouts, and the title not only refers to the old cockney saying for something truly strange but moreover a thing appearing natural that is really unnatural.

Screenwriter Terry Southern first gave Kubrick a copy of Burgess' controversial 1962 novel during the making of *2001: A Space Odyssey*. Kubrick picked it up one evening and read it in one sitting. "By the end of Part One it seemed pretty obvious that it might make a great film," he later remembered. "By the end of Part Two I was very excited about it. As soon as I finished it, I immediately reread it. For the next two or three days, I reread it in whole and in part, and did little else but think about it."

Written in exquisite, exotic Nadsat, a futuristic teenage dialect redolent with Russian and nonsense words (Burgess had been in Russia and witnessed two gangs of hooligans tangle outside a cafe where they incorporated English slang into their vitriol), the novel took Kubrick on a journey through a violence-ridden totalitarian society with a fifteen year-old English malchick (guy) named Alex and his droogs (mates) Pete, Georgie, and Dim. After peeting (drinking) moloko with knives in it (milk laced with hallucinogens and amphetamines with names like vellocet, synthemesc, and drencrom) at the Korova Milkbar to "sharpen you up and make you ready for a bit of dirty twenty-to-one [ultraviolence]," the boys go out into the nochy (night) and viddy (see) just

whom they might crast (rob) of a bit of pretty polly (money) or tolchock to snuff (beat to death), or just engage in a bit of the old in-out-in-out (rape).

In turns of phrase alternately Elizabethan, cutesylike, and all viciousylike, Alex relates "O my brothers" how his molodoy moodges (young men), attired in tights with the old jelly mould (designer codpieces), waistcoats with huge pletchoes (shoulders), off-white cravats, and flip horrorshow (wildly good) boots for kicking, spend their evening. The game plan includes sobirating a ded pyanhista (accosting an old wino) and practically oobivating (killing) him with kicks to the gutiwats and gulliver (stomach and head). They break in on the gang rape of a creeching, nagoy devotchka (screaming, naked young girl). With nazh and oozy (knife and chain) they osoosh (wipe) the floor with the other shaika (gang), spilling a malenky krovvy (little blood) and ookadeeting (leaving) before the millicents (police) arrive at the bitva (battle).

After skvatting (grabbing) a car, the droogs yeckate skorry (drive quickly) into the nearby country for a bit of "the olde surprise visit." Using the imploringly earnest ruse of needing a phone for a car accident victim, they

burst, masked and smecking (laughing), into the home of a middle-aged writer chelloveck (man) and his young zheena (wife). Alex's droogs make "his litso [face] all purple and dripping away like some very special sort of juicy fruit." They vred his plott (damage his body) so badly he'll never gooly (walk) again, tape his rot (mouth), and make him witness the strack (horror) of them shiving off the sharp's platties (slicing off the woman's clothes) and plunging (raping) her one after the other. Then they trash the rest of the apartment (including a book the writer is writing, called *A Clockwork Orange*) before Alex calls, "Out out out out," sending

OPPOSITE: Alex and his droogs pay a housecall and prepare to indulge in a bit of the old in-out in Stanley Kubrick's chilling **A Clockwork Orange.** *ABOVE: Flanked by Dim (left) and Georgie (right), Alex (Malcolm McDowell) has had his fill of "moloko with knives in it" (druglaced milk) and is ready for a night of ultra violence in* **A Clockwork Orange.**

them speeding back to town, "running over odd squealing things on the way."

The night has only begun. Alex's adventures in wonderland come to an end when his authority-chaffed droogs set him up for a big fall. He goes to the Staja (State Jail) for fourteen years to be prisoner #6655321 shut up in a "grahzny [dirty] hellhole and like human zoo...being kicked and tolchocked by brutal bully warders and meeting vonny [smelly] leering like criminals, some of them real perverts and ready to dribble all over a luscious young malchick like your story-teller."

So inspired, Alex becomes a model prisoner, befriending the charlie (chaplain) and burying himself in the Bog's book (the Bible), mostly to read the raskazz (stories) of pol (sex) and ultraviolence while strains of his favorite Ludwig van (Beethoven) run through his mozg (brain). When an opportunity comes to cut his sentence by volunteering for the experimental Ludovico's Technique (a brutal behavioral modification regimen to render him incapable of violence or sexual aggression), he jumps at it with radosty (joy) and lands right in hell. Ludovico's Technique works and Alex returns to a wicked world for some very different adventures with the sickest of twists before he's through.

Kubrick was blown away by this masterwork. He effused, "The narrative invention was magical, the characters were bizarre and exciting, the ideas were brilliantly developed, and equally important, the story was of a size and density that could be adapted to film without oversimplifying it or stripping it to the bones." Usually a glutton for research (he read sixty to seventy tomes on nuclear weapons and interviewed rocket scientists for *Dr. Strangelove*, 1964), the director did minimal research in behavioral psychology and conditioned reflex-therapy, and set about finding ways to communicate the weird way Burgess set up his world without quite all the lingo that was bound to lose audiences.

The answer was sound and vision. Kubrick did the part he liked best, preparation, for as he says, "Shooting is the part of filmmaking that I enjoy the least. I don't particularly enjoy working

BELOW: *Little Alex (Malcom McDowell) has nothing to hide as he goes into serve time for a little rape and murder in* **A Clockwork Orange.**

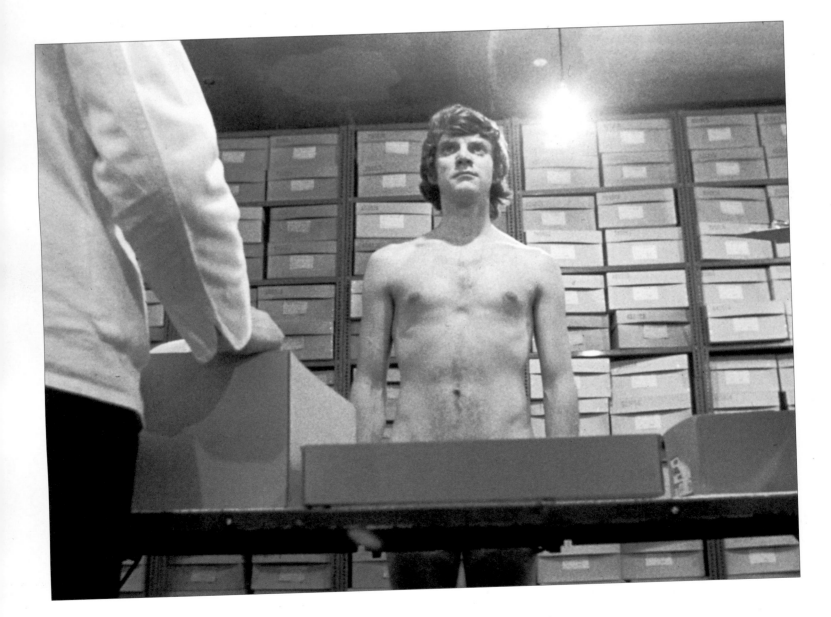

with a lot of people. I'm just not an extrovert." For weeks, he and production designer John Barry scanned architectural magazines for suitable settings. An art exhibition displaying female figures as furniture gave him the disturbing decor (mannequins doing gymnastic bridges as tables, breasts dispensing drugged milk) of the Korova.

To match the poetry of Alex's narration in the book, Kubrick turned to music (as he had in *2001*). Exquisite Elgar, Purcell, Rossini, Korsakoff, and of course Ludwig van would lilt tongue in cheek as blood flowed from many a mouth. Balletic violence would make *Bonnie and Clyde* (1967) look clumsy. Inspired by listening to Mozart's peppy *Eine Kleine Nachtmusik*, Kubrick scored the "William Tell Overture" to a forty-second, high-speed orgy between Alex and two girls (in the book they're ten years old) whom he picks up in a record store (shot at two frames per second, the action is really twenty-eight minutes long).

Kubrick had the technical expertise to match his poetic side. Wide-angle lenses could make a small space look cavernous. Other lenses requiring very little light shot urban squalor without dimming out, and interiors were lit almost exclusively with quartz bulbs in the real lamps and lights on the set (making complete camera pans possible). A Super-mica microphone, the size of a paper clip, made the drunk's dialogue under the busy Albert Bridge so clear that traffic noise had to be added in.

There were some changes from the book, but not many. The droogs would look different. In addition to the codpieces, Kubrick added white overalls, bowler hats, and, for Alex, false eyelashes for one eye. It is an extreme close-up of that leering face that we linger on after the simple credits roll by. Kubrick knew Alex had to have all the villainous charm of Richard III and had had only one actor's voice in his brain ever since the book's second chapter. After having seen Lindsay Anderson's British boys' school nightmare, *if....* (1968), he knew Malcolm McDowell's aura of both intelligence and animal instinct were Alex incarnate.

"With Alex, you're not so much playing a character as this force," the actor acknowledged. After choosing a Lancashire accent over the harsher cockney, McDowell was unleashed into Burgess' nightmare during the CRP (Crucial Rehearsal Period) for every scene. "This period is one of maximum tension and anxiety," Kubrick adds, "and it is precisely here where a scene lives or dies. The choice of camera angles and coverage is, by comparison, a relatively simple matter." In one such rehearsal, where Alex kicks the writer around the room before violating his wife, Kubrick asked his young star if he could sing and dance. As the only song the actor could recall all the words to was Gene Kelly's "Singin' in the Rain" number from the 1952 film of the same name. McDowell tried out the tune in between bestial acts and Kubrick got an assistant on the transatlantic phone to buy the rights. A piece of movie history was born.

That was the easy part. Kubrick, the notorious eccentric (he won't ride as a passenger if the car is going more than thirty miles per hour [48kph] and has a wardrobe of only blue blazers, gray slacks, and black shoes to save time on clothes choice), was also a notorious perfectionist. For a scene where Alex's social worker spit in his face, it took twenty-five takes before the gob hung just where he wanted it to, on McDowell's lower lip. Likewise, Ludovico's Technique required McDowell's eyelids to be held permanently open in a metal harness. Real anesthetic had to be continually flushed over the actor's orbs. Held face down in a trough of freezing muck (bullion) for several minutes by his old chums, now members of the police department, McDowell had to be hooked up to an air hose to prevent him from drowning. And in the scene where they beat him, crushed ribs and torn chest cartilage resulted in three weeks of downtime while McDowell healed.

The film was a sensation. Alex's ultraviolent travels as the scourge and ultimately the tool of an increasingly totalitarian society won the praise of fellow filmmakers like Luis Bunuel, Akira Kurosawa, and Federico Fellini, as well as four Oscar nominations, the New York Film Critics' Award for best film and director, the Hugo Award for best sci-fi film of 1971, and prestigious Italian, Belgian, and German awards.

It also won the condemnation of many. Though British censors passed it for audiences eighteen and older, tensions in 1971 between rival Mod and Rocker gangs flared from the release. In Lancashire, a young woman was raped by a gang of youths singin' "Singin' in the Rain," while elsewhere a sixteen-year-old wearing a bowler, white overalls, and combat boots kicked another kid nearly to death. Finally, Kubrick and Warner Bros. withdrew it from distribution in England, where it remained banned for nineteen years—until finally released just in time for the book's actual time setting, O my brothers.

THANKS FOR THE MEMORIES, OR, ARNOLD SAVES THE DAY!

What if nothing, no human activity, is safe? With every other aspect of the future a potential horror, it's only right that pleasure and pastimes be made menacing. Maybe it's work-ethic guilt over too much leisure time. Maybe it's the thrill of the innocent made deadly. Maybe it's fear of travel. Almost everyone has heard the urban myth of the nest of rattlesnakes left undetected in the amusement park roller-coaster car, only to be discovered by a happy family of tourists during the middle of their first (and last) ride of the summer. That ain't nothin' over what can happen in a hundred years or so.

In 1951, the same year he wrote the classic science fiction novel *The Illustrated Man*, Ray Bradbury spun a sinister little story called "The Veldt" about a couple of apple-cheeked, marble-eyed tykes whose addiction to

> "Just because you're paranoid doesn't mean they're not out to get you."
>
> —old saying

their high-tech nursery (which can morph its crystal walls, floor, and ceiling to replicate any environment on Earth) outlives their parents. When George Hadley tries to take a firm hand with his children and shut down the room, Peter and Wendy lock their parents in their African plains playroom, which proves to be so real that mom and dad are ripped apart by lions.

The Most Dangerous Game (1932) did for hunting what *Deliverance* (1972) did for canoeing and what *Jaws* (1975) did for swimming and fishing and waterskiing and snorkeling. Recreation of all kinds has been vilified from the most raucous

carnival carnage in *The Funhouse* (1981) right down to sedate shuffleboard in *The Poseidon Adventure* (1972). And as far as sightseeing, *Jurassic Park* (1993) took a bite out of that thrill. Face it—at play you are just not safe.

No, Arnold Schwarzenegger is not delivering a baby, but something much more vital, the future of the planet Mars in the totally amazing **Total Recall** *(1990).*

Finally, since memories are the most cherished component of any recreation, science fiction has had its way with them, too. Films like *Brainstorm* and *Strange Days* (1995) made vagaries of vicarious living more up close and personal by showing nasty, addictive recording devices that allowed personal experience from sex to murder to heart attacks and death to be used and abused by a voyeur wearing the right headset.

The wildest premise is that vacation memories can be completely synthetic. Master science fiction writer Phillip K. Dick, who had previously fabricated whole personal histories for highly advanced humanity-starved robots in his 1968 novel *Do Androids Dream of Electric Sheep?* (which was later adapted into the grim visionary film *Blade Runner*), merged characteristics of James Thurber's nebbish short-story hero Walter Mitty and James Bond to create another future earthling with memories of a double life (or insanity) in the 1987 short story "We Can Remember It For You Wholesale." It's 2048 and construction worker Douglas Quaid has been having unexplainable yearnings to go to the Mars frontier, where an oppressive mining operation and an enslaved, oxygen-regulated colony of workers have long been in place. He's so hungry for adventure that he's been having uncomfortably realistic dreams of space-espionage adventures on the red planet with a female companion. Driving his wife, Lori, and coworkers nuts with his inexplicable obsession, he opts for a recreational remedy to his problem.

Since his spouse would rather die than vacation on the arid, airless sphere, Quaid goes to Rekall Inc., where for a heap of credits (money to us) he can have the recollection of a customized vacation there (complete with a "brunette, athletic, sleazy" companion) implanted in his brain—memories to last a lifetime.

That might not be so very long. Something goes very wrong during the memory implantation process and Quaid goes berzerk. In near-convulsions, Quaid is seized upon by the conviction that his life is in imminent danger from assassins and that he is not the humdrum, blue-collar bozo he thought he was, but a secret agent named Houser who needs to get back to Mars to stop a corporate cutthroat named Cohaagen (who brainwashed Houser into Quaid when he turned against him) from exterminating a rebel leader among the mine workers named Kuato. Revelation or delusion, he doesn't have much time for analysis (a psychiatrist will try to do that later).

Houser's date and ex duke it out in **Total Recall.** *Arnold admired Rachel Ticotin's (left) rough-and-tumble attitude but was less enthused about Sharon Stone's (right) care with her hair during fight scenes.*

When hit men led by a maniac named Richter try to waste him on the way home, he discovers catlike defense reflexes he never knew he possessed. When his wife tries to seduce him into his hunters' clutches, she blurts out that his whole life with her is just a memory implant and tries to kill him herself. When a mysterious stranger (claiming to be a former fellow agent) hands him a suitcase that includes not only his old identity papers but a videotaped message from his former self (yes, this is getting tricky here) begging him to get to Mars, even showing him how to extract the bulbous tracking device that is implanted in his nose, he takes the next space shuttle for you-know-where.

Not bad for a beginning, which is exactly what screenwriter Roland Shussett thought when he optioned the story. Yet it was sixteen years before it became a reality. Teaming up to write *Total Recall* (1990) with Dan O'Bannon, who had cowritten John Carpenter's darkly comic *Dark Star* (1974), Shussett took on another project with his partner, a little something called *Alien* (1979). After getting no more than fifteen pages done on *Total Recall*, O'Bannon was recalled to Paris for a year, where he was to hammer out the script for *Dune* (1984). Shussett was so despondent that his wife, Linda, took him to her pastor, who told him to expect "a miracle" within two weeks. Miraculously, the phone soon rang, and with *Dune* on hold, O'Bannon announced that he was headed stateside.

O'Bannon bunked with the Shussetts while he and Roland hammered out *Alien*, which grossed $125 million worldwide and made them a very hot property. The *Recall* script was not so easy. Still, though the final third was missing (the script was circulated with a note reading, "The loose ends will be tied together and the rest of the film will work perfectly"), Disney took the bait and optioned, which ran out without a production. Next, Dino DeLaurentiis' daughter Raffaella took a shine to it and peddled it to her pop, who from 1981 to 1988 tried to sell the script (while fifty drafts were done to resolve the weak ending) to directors including Fred Schepisi, Russell Mulcahy, Lewis Teague, and David Cronenberg.

The Canadian horror master Cronenberg signed on, got set to shoot in Rome, wrangled with distributor MGM over the huge budget, acquiesced to name actor Richard Dreyfuss as the lead but

Quaid (Arnold) has the power drill and someone is going to get screwed as he fights for Mars' freedom in the climax of **Total Recall.**

rebelled at the command to tailor the script to the actor's perky persona, wanted a darker ending, and dropped out of the project. It was back to square one. DeLaurentiis demanded that the expensive Mars setting be dropped. "Make it action-oriented like *Rambo*," he told Shussett (O'Bannon had by this time given up on the seemingly doomed venture). "Go to a foreign country, kill a lot of people." But the writer wouldn't budge, broke off contact with the mogul, and set about crafting a satisfactory last third with the help of Steven Pressfield. The real or imagined manhunt for Quaid would escalate on Mars where, aided by a Venusville (Mars' red-

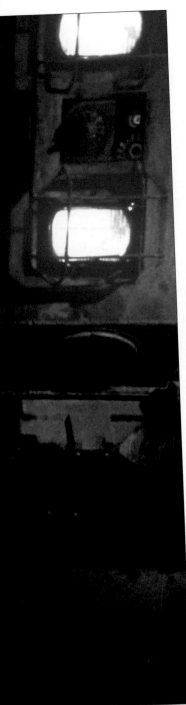

light district) prostitute named Melina, in a sea of exotic mutants, he would both uncover a wonderful secret left deep within the planet by the long-departed Martians and become the victim of an almost unimaginable betrayal.

Eventually DeLaurentiis got director Bruce Beresford hot to do the improved project, but couldn't get the news through to Shussett. "I didn't want the stress of talking to Dino," Shussett admitted. "He'd been offering me $100,000, $200,000 to agree to take out Mars. I thought, 'He's going to go up to a million dollars and I'll make myself sick by saying no.'" But the message that Dino finally got through was, "Mars is back. I love you so much I could kiss you on the mouth." Patrick Swayze was set to play Quaid and sets were soon being built in Australia. Then in 1988, two months before principal photography, the DeLaurentiis' Company went belly up and doom descended. *Total Recall* was totally dead. Or was it?

Muscle in Austrian bodybuilding champ Arnold Schwarzenegger, who had cannily been making the transition from hulk to action hunk to actor. Arnold had read the script four years earlier and loved the possibility of playing a normal guy in extraordinary circumstances but didn't have the clout to get it done his own careful way with approval on everything. Now, with *Red Heat* (1988) a smash hit for the Carolco Company; his recent comic outing, *Twins* (1988), proving that even Bavarian muscle men had a lovable side; and the enthusiasm of *RoboCop*'s (1987) Dutch sci-fi-action director, Paul Verhoeven, to collaborate, he had the power. One call from Arnold to Carolco instructing "Pay the turnaround no matter how many millions it costs" turned what Shussett had termed "an Egyptian curse" into a blessed nightmare of the future for the masses.

Total Recall is a totally high-tech, maniacally violent yet psychologically probing totalitarian tale complete with gritty, unglamorous settings (ten huge soundstages housing forty-five sets) for a brutalized Earth and a marred Mars (all shot in Mexico City over 130 grueling days) and enough futuristic features to make a person's eyes bug out. Makeup designer Rob Bottin incorporated animatronic effects including "details such as re-creating the movements of muscles under the skin or inserting little tubes to allow saliva or drool" in the movie's creatures. Made by combining "makeup, controls, gears, servos, electronics, and optics," the

effects took a full seven months to develop. Thanks to "real-time motion control photography" (allowing minute camera movements to be exactly replicated by computer for coinciding special effects shots), Dream Quest Images was able to shoot one hundred bluescreen shots, including gigantic forty- by sixty-foot (12 by 18m) model cityscapes right alongside live counterparts. In this future both the familiar and the fantastic abound. It's a dystopia of hologramic tennis coaches, android cab drivers, skeleton-revealing airport security systems, menacing mine-digging equipment, and subways slashing through Martian canals.

Gore abounds as well. *Total Recall* literally drips with it, but there's chemistry in this plasma. Verhoeven, the math and physics doctorate-toting madman prone to multitake perfectionism, and Schwarzenegger, the cigar-chomping, jovial bastion of Republican sanity, make an awesome director/star team. The Dutch director's family was bombed by the Nazis from the time he was two years old until he was seven. "I remember sitting at the table with my parents having dinner, and whole windows would blow in our face, because there's a bomb in the next house....My brain has been involved with violence when I was a kid so much that when I close my eyes, I see burning houses," he said. Conversely, Schwarzenegger was always so Aryanly developed that he spent a lifetime being polite and even-tempered to reassure people that his muscles meant no harm. "I was always better with lovey-dovey talk than with dialogue when I'm mad and angry," the ex–Mister Universe says.

With his superstar clout, Arnold kept Carolco from squelching Verhoeven's crimson-tinted vision of the future (so bloody that his crew wore garbage bags to protect themselves from flying flesh and blood) while hoping along with everyone else that the director would stop short of an X rating. "I don't care what it takes," Schwarzenegger offers. "You can scream at me, call me for a shot at midnight, keep me waiting for four hours. As long as what ends up on the screen is perfect."

Total Recall comes pretty close and leaves the Powders, Crows, Batmen, Johnny Mnemonics, and other denizens of the *Strange Days* to come choking in the Martian dust. Sure, bad guys are reamed with gigantic screws (giving Arnold one of his signature lines for the film, "Screw you!"). Wife Lori (Sharon Stone) and Martian rebel Melina (Rachel Ticotin) engage in mortal combat most men would buckle at.

Faces explode. Arms are chopped off at the elbow. Whole bodies are split up the middle. A corpse is used as a bullet-riddled human shield. Yet amid the howls for blood and the mind-blowing special effects (Mars undergoes some major changes by the end) is a more detailed and unpleasantly credible dystopia than has ever been brought to the screen. As futures go, *Total Recall*'s seems far too close. And what it has to say about Quaid's adolescent espionage fantasies is the same writing on the cinema wall that all good future shock movies maintain: beware of what you wish for, for you may surely get it. And it just might be much more than you're ready for.

Chapter Four

TIME TRIPPING

We shall not cease from exploration
And the end of all our exploring
Will be to arrive where we started
And know the place for the first time.

—from "Gerontion," by T.S. Eliot

Bruce Willis does a little recon-
naissance above ground prior
to time-tripping back to before
the world was one big bio-haz-
ard in 12 Monkeys *(1995)*.

Songster Steve Miller is right—"Time keeps on slippin' into the future." Ever since what astrophysicists like to call the first "singularity" (an infinite denseness and compression of all matter and space) burst, the universe has been moving out in three physical dimensions and moving right along in a nonphysical fourth time.

Egyptian pharaohs sought to monumentally outlast it. Mayan astronomers studied and worshiped it. Since humankind's imagination first soared beyond survival, we have been fascinated by time's deliciously abstract possibilities. After immortality and human flight, what could be more marvelous than traveling beyond the here and now? Who hasn't daydreamed of jumping back in time to meet a legend like Beethoven, Cleopatra, or Christ? Who hasn't had a hankering to take a peek at the marvels of the next millennium?

Time-tripping in fiction has always been a favorite, whether forward or backward. Like the hero of Washington Irving's 1819 story "Rip Van Winkle," you might just snooze your way (the cheapest form of suspended animation) into the future and miss the American Revolution in the process. Or, like the blacksmith from Mark Twain's 1889 *A Connecticut Yankee in King Arthur's Court*, you could dream yourself into the past to impress the locals with your visionary grasp of technology. Like all-American dentist Billy Pilgrim, from Kurt Vonnegut's masterpiece *Slaughterhouse-Five*; you might find yourself flipping between Dresden, Germany; Illium, New York; and the planet Tralfamadore without any control. But with the right time machine the world could be your oyster. You could even be able to change the future by dipping into the past.

In an August 1996 article in *Smithsonian Magazine*, American notables were asked what they would do if they could travel in a time machine. Their answers were as diverse as sharing Meriwether Lewis' first view of the Continental Divide (President Bill Clinton), playing against Lou Gehrig (Cal Ripken, Jr.), seeing the geologic shaping of the earth (Maya Lin), being in on the invention of the transistor (Bill Gates), exploring the Galapagos Islands with Charles Darwin (Gary Larson), eating lobster with Plymouth Rock pilgrims (Julia Child), and witnessing the impact of that Tunguska meteor in Siberia (Chuck Yeager). Everybody wants to travel in time, and science fiction writers and directors are no exception.

The silent era took a relatively ridiculing look at time travel with films like *One Hundred Years After* (1911), in which a Thomas Edison–like character places himself in a state of suspended animation and is held for a century in a safe deposit box at Harvard University, only to awaken to a society run by (perish the thought) women. Thanks to his expert lovemaking, the mayoress of New York is convinced to give men the right to vote. The tide turned to romance in early talkies like *Berkeley Square* (1933), in which a freak accident sends scientist Leslie Howard, who is obsessed with the eighteenth century, back to 1783 to impersonate one of his ancestors and fall in love with his distant cousin. By the wisecracking forties things were more comic than cosmic. In *Where Do We Go from Here?* (1945) frustrated 4-F army reject Fred MacMurray finds a magic lamp that grants his enlistment wish but sends him back to George Washington's regiment. It took time for time travel to be taken seriously.

DIALING FOR DINOS

As tempting as the future is, the past is something we know about and we have the fossils to prove it. Even more exciting than exchanging grunts with Neolithic man, traveling back to the Jurassic period for a firsthand peek at the "thunder lizards" is a fantasy that appealed to youthful minds long before Michael Crichton and Steven Spielberg took the dino craze to its inevitable extreme. Time travel with a budget might not afford such a primeval perambulation, but if the creatures happen to be tucked away in a remote pocket of the present (from Loch Ness to Andean plateaus), then why not go there?

This was the thought that occurred to one of science fiction film's models of special effects expertise, Willis O'Brien. His paleontological predilection began when he was a trapper and guide in Oregon's wilderness, taking scientists to Crater Lake (an unearthly blue body of water sitting in a mile [1.6km]-wide volcanic crater) to look for fossils. Later, as a newspaper cartoonist, O'Brien started doodling dinos. Working the San Francisco World's Fair of 1914 and molding a boxer out of clay, he took his inspiration from popular flip-books and borrowed a newsreel camera. This would lead him to virtually pioneer what we now call stop-motion photography by bringing his boxer to life.

By 1914 O'Brien had made a five-minute film that took two painstaking months to shoot, *The Dinosaur and the Missing Link*. He went back to the Stone Age again, featuring an apatosaurus (cousin of the brontosaurus) in *The Birth of a Flivver* (1916). *Morpheus Mike* (1917) depicted an opium-induced dream of cavemen with the protagonist munching mammoths for dinner and working as a mailman in an (R.F.D. Rural Federal District) 10,000 B.C. *The Ghost of Slumber Mountain* (1919) gave a crazed hermit a starscope by which he could view his woodsy abode in past millennia. Film's first special effects wizard was on his way.

By 1922, Sir Arthur Conan Doyle's celebrated adventure novel *The Lost World* was almost in the hands of Burbank, California's First National production company. Harry Hoyt was slated to direct the tale of the wild and woolly Professor George Edward Challenger (the book describes him alternately as "a homicidal maniac with a turn for science" and "the best-hated man in London") and his trip to an isolated plateau high in the Andes where dinosaurs still rule and ape-men don't evolve. Along with a scoffing academic named Summerlee (Arthur Hoyt), a spoiled sportsman named Roxton (Lewis Stone), a newshound named Malone (Lloyd Hughes), and an added love interest, Paula White (Bessie Love), Challenger (the incomparably burly Wallace Beery) would bring back a brontosaurus to be displayed in London, where naturally it would run amok before swimming

*Professor Challenger's little artifact from **The Lost World** runs amok in London in one of the first and finest dino-flicks ever.*

In Jurassic Park, *time travel is not an option as dinosaurs are brought to life in the twentieth century.*

and bony plates. Air bladders in the models simulated breathing. Shellac doubled for dino drool. Chocolate syrup stood in for blood during dino fights. What prehistoric locale the L.A. River could not provide, a huge in-studio tank housing miniature thatched huts and canoes did.

Director of photography Arthur Edeson exposed two frames per crank of his camera, with a mere thirty seconds of finished film the usual output of a day's work. Control was the watchword. Flickerless Cooper Hewitt mercury vapor lights ensured crucial lighting consistency from frame to frame. Ralph Hameras' ingenious shots through glass whose edges were carefully painted replaced the need for many elaborate sets. On the big end of things the movie could boast only a life-size bronto tail by which humans could be knocked about. Everything else looked big but was built little. Panoramic prehistoric vistas sprouted miniature grass in ten days. London streets could be destroyed with wires tucked inside ready-to-crumble miniature buildings. And after nothing less than a volcanic eruption, a stampede of various dinos lasting a full five minutes (edited down to a mere minute and a half) flooded the screen.

Studio execs may have had a contingency plan, but O'Brien and Delgado accomplished the impossible. *The Lost World* (1925) not only made O'Brien a hero and king of sci-fi special effects for years to come, but it was such a smash with audiences that it was the first in-flight movie for the German Air Service Company. *The Lost World* would hatch a host of timeless dino movies in years to

home (in the novel, a pterodactyl egg hatches and flies away instead).

Hoyt knew just who to contact about populating his frozen past with dinosaurs. O'Brien had been attending classes at the Los Angeles Art Institute, where he recruited a talented nineteen-year-old Mexican immigrant, classmate Marcel Delgado, to be his chief model-making assistant. Together with Hoyt, they made a test reel to convince Doyle to sell the rights to his book. It wowed the author so much that he borrowed the reel in June 1922 to impress his fellow members of the American Society of Magicians (which included Harry Houdini).

Given the green light, Hoyt, O'Brien, Delgado, and company set out on a grueling fourteen months of filming for ninety minutes of silent film. The modelers started by poring over the dino paintings of Charles R. Knight at the American Natural History Museum in New York. Back in Los Angeles they constructed detailed models twelve inches (30.5cm) high and sixteen to twenty inches (41 to 51cm) long. Pieces of sponge and wood provided the underbody with a con-

come with ever-increasing sophistication to their modeling. From giants like *King Kong* (1931) (for which Willis O'Brien headed the special effects crew) and *Jurassic Park* (1993) to lesser films like *The Lost Continent* (1951), *The Land That Time Forgot* (1975) (based on Tarzan creator Edgar Rice Burroughs' novel), and *Baby...Secret of the Lost Legend* (1985), all paleontological past-meets-present premises follow in the fossilized footsteps of this wonderful movie.

necting network of wire overlayed for movement. Clay filled in as flesh while rubber sheeting from dental dams snapped to as horns

ABOVE: O'Brien's masterpiece was that great ape, here holding Fay Wray above the New York skyline, King Kong *(1931).*

CLASSIC COME TO LIFE

Legendary science fiction producer/director George Pal wasn't the first person to want to adapt H.G. Wells' classic novella of time travel for the viewing public. Shortly after the 1895 publication of *The Time Machine*, inventor Robert W. Paul approached the author with the idea of a multimedia version of the work complete with slides, film, live actors, and lighting effects. Wells agreed. Paul secured a patent but never went through with it. We can hardly blame his ambition or his failure.

Who wouldn't want to visualize a first-person narrative that would fling its inventor hero from turn-of-the-century London to a dreamy but deadly new Eden in the postapocalyptic year 802701 and, finally, to the uncanny twilight of life itself on Earth and the fade out of our sun? Who wouldn't be baffled at how to match a

book that gave detailed driver's-seat descriptions of what it was like to hear, feel, and see time flood and metamorphose around you? Pal's success in 1953 with Wells' *The War of the Worlds* sent the director rifling through the master's other works and deciding on this untried (except for an unsuccessful BBC television adaptation in 1949) gem of a novella. Luckily for all of us, Wells' son Frank liked Pal's previous adaptation well enough to offer him a steal of an option. Pal jumped at the chance.

With David Duncan assisting him with the screenplay, Pal remained relatively true to Wells' story. The traveler (nameless in the novel and dubbed George in the screenplay) would demonstrate a small-scale model of his time machine to his intellectual

Rod Taylor as "the time traveller" readies himself for a take-off that will launch him fantastically far from Victorian England in The Time Machine.

cronies over cigars and brandy. Irked by their disbelief, he would
hop into the full-scale model after their departure and lurch unprepared and unprovisioned into a future he hoped would be enlight-
ened. There, he would meet the fragile, childlike, technology-lacking
Eloi (among them his love interest, Weena), whose seemingly bliss-
ful existence among the paradisiacal ruins of past civilization
would lead to dark questions.

Who provided their food and clothes? Why were they terrified
of the dark? What were those strange passageways going deep
into the earth; the sinister clanging that sounded from their depths;
the albino bodies, glowing eyes, groping hands, and insidious
intent lurking in their darkness? What Pavlovian nightmare would
begin when those Morlocks set the ancient air-raid siren next to the
open doors of the stone sphinx to shrieking?

Unlike the book, Pal's script dodged the end-of-time scenario
and added a romantic ending to Wells' story that Hollywood

should have drooled over. Still, it wasn't until he proved his bank-
ability to MGM with the release of his fantasy *tom thumb* (1958) that
Pal got the green light and an $825,000 budget for *The Time
Machine* (1960). The director was a genuine believer in the possibility of time travel and claimed that his belief helped his film
immensely. So did his vast experience with stop-motion animation.

George's journey through time amid the spacial confines of
his lab—with flowers blooming at high speed, a snail speeding
across the floor, sun and moon racing across the sky, unseen hands
streaming a fashion parade on a mannequin viewed through his
window, and the very walls of his laboratory crumbling down and
the landscape outside transforming before our eyes—would easily
earn this movie and Pal's old stop-action compadres, Wah Chang
and Gene Warren, an Oscar for Special Effects. Chang's accelerat-
ed decomposition of one of the Morlock masters by stop-action
stripping of layers of futuristic anatomy from a human skeleton is
especially eerie.

To make the time travel even more believable to a nuke-con-
scious sixties audience, a stop or two was added to the trip. Though
he tinkered with the idea of updating the setting, as he had with
The War of the Worlds, Pal instead added scenes where the travel-

er drops in just after World War I to mistake a young soldier for the
boy's late father and where he witnesses the 1962 nuking of London
complete with lava erupting from the earth (made of red-dyed oatmeal), which he barely escapes.

The machine itself is an elegant flight of Victorian fancy with
a modern twist. Nothing is overtly high-tech here, but as Pal

ABOVE: *That way luncheon lies...and lunch is you! Try telling that to a bunch of future farm-fed Eloi. The time traveller and Weena (Yvette Mimieux) try to stop the slaughter in the caves of the Morlocks. OPPOSITE: One Morlock likes his lunch (in this case, Weena) on the run in* The Time Machine.

remembers, "The design all started with a barber chair. Bill Ferrari, the art director, thought that was a good way to begin....Then he came up with the idea for a sledlike design. He sketched that out and I liked it. And then we put the controls in the front. I thought it was a good idea. He sketched, and I sketched, and other people made comments. And then Bill said we needed something behind it to indicate movement. So he came up with the big, radarlike wheel." The radar-sled is a beauty in any century and the inscription glimpsed on it, "Manufactured by H. George Wells," is an equally elegant touch.

Though Shakespearean star Paul Scofield was first pick for George, and Michael Rennie and James Mason were both possibilities, American unknown Rod Taylor (who would later appear in Hitchcock's *The Birds*, 1963) is admirable as the dashing idealist who is as macho as he is articulate. Newcomer Yvette Mimieux is appropriately otherworldly and innocent, and even Alan Young as George's beleaguered best friend is head and forelocks above his later work in television's *Mister Ed*. *The Time Machine* is a timeless treat not to be missed.

EVERY PRIMATE HAS ITS DAY

Ham (the astronaut chimp who was sent into suborbit in 1961), Koko (a gorilla who knows American Sign Language), and Washoe (a similarly inclined chimp with a 130-sign vocabulary) have all shown that intelligence may not be *Homo sapiens'* eminent domain. But who's to say that if the evolutionary dice had been thrown differently, other primates might not now have supremacy?

ABOVE: Captain Taylor (Charlton Heston) indulges in an inter-species embrace with a chimp named Zira (Kim Hunter) at the climax of* Planet of the Apes *(1968).

Such was the radical concept of Pierre Boulle's satirical novel about a futuristic couple named Jinn and Phyllis on a space vacation. The couple finds a distress message in a bottle from Ulysse Merou, a journalist who accompanied a landing on an earthlike planet in the year 2500 only to discover a very different social order. From this novel came the first Hollywood movie to keep a $75,000 budget for human hair, wig makers busy for three months before filming, and the majority of its large cast at the makeup table for more than four hours a day.

Planet of the Apes (1968)—is it a parable about racial oppression, animal rights, human arrogance, and the dangers of technology, or is it just an eyeful of entertainment with a premise so startling that we can't take our eyes off the screen? Whatever it is, it became a sci-fi milestone and "evolved" into no less than three sequels a decade before a *Star Wars* (1977) logo ever graced a lunch box.

The plot is simple. A team of four astronauts—a brilliant female scientist, a dedicated biologist, an idealistic patriot, and a cynical and supremely arrogant captain—takes off from Earth in 1979 for a planet in the Orion constellation. Their voyage in suspended animation while traveling near the speed of light is designed to age them only a few months and put them seven hundred years into the future, but something goes terribly wrong. Their ship doesn't land, but crashes and sinks into water on a seemingly lifeless planet (actually Page, Arizona, and Utah's Lake Powell). Their lady scientist, Landon, is a withered corpse in her suspension chamber. The calendar reads not 2679 but 3978.

Trekking across this barren landscape of rock is bad enough for the three bearded survivors (Jeff Burton, playing the patriotic Dodge, fainted in the desert heat the very first day of shooting). While skinny-dipping in the first water they find, their clothes are stolen by

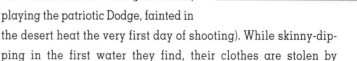

In **Escape from Planet of the Apes** *(1971) it was the primates' turn to time travel from their shattered world to present-day U.S.A.
Their welcome would be no warmer than what we humans got from their cohorts in the original.*

WHEN AM I THIS TIME?

Sit down and strap yourself in. Set all the gauges, levers, dials, crystals, and chronometers. Now it's your turn to do the millennium mambo. We're going to send you to some way-out places, so get ready to time-trip and see if you can tell us what movies you've just become the star of.

YOU ARE

1. H.G. himself tracking down your old pal Jack the Ripper in 1970s San Francisco.

2. a killer from 2586 having a heck of a time with your .357 Magnum back in the Old West. Your only worry is a pesky college professor.

3. back in the Old West with your chopper, gettin' ready to lay rubber and clean up a dirty town.

4. in the company of six dwarfs (but you're pretty short yourself) trying to patch things up with Robin Hood, King Agamemnon, and Napoleon.

5. going to "most heinously" flunk out of high school unless you get Joan of Arc, Billy the Kid, Genghis Kahn, and honest Abe for your oral history report.

6. off with your granddaughters to the future and the planet Skaro to save the Thals from a robot menace guided by a gelatinous mass of intensified brain power.

7. off where no humpbacks have ever gone before—1970s San Francisco to save the planet with whale song.

8. on a very strange shore leave as your 1943 battleship passes into 1984, thanks to your navy's clumsy radar cloaking.

9. on a new beat, back from 2247 Angel City to 1985 Los Angeles to stop a time-traveling mystic and his zombies.

10. in love with an old photo of a turn-of-the-century actress, so why not go back to 1912 Michigan for a tragic tryst.

11. an ancient alien embedded in a pharaoh's mummy and reactivated by X-rays three thousand years later.

12. on the USS Nimitz and, thanks to a strange storm, tossed back to 1941 to take part in Pearl Harbor.

13. a failed suicide who gets to travel back in a womblike blob to try to get it right the second time.

14. fleeing Cumbria and the Black Plague of 1348 only to tunnel through the center of the earth to 1989 New Zealand.

15. a neurotic twentieth-century Greenwich Village health food store owner who has been brought two hundred years forward thanks to a botched ulcer operation.

16. on a mission to 1955 to direct Dad out of nerddom and maybe change the course of rock 'n' roll forever.

17. a race driver who has crashed eighteen years into the future thanks to a dying tycoon who wants your body for his own.

18. a wisecracking, wicked weatherman tripped up in Punxsutawney, Pennsylvania, for what may be the rest of eternity—one same day at a time.

19. an erring knight errant who, to unkill your father-in-law, has mistakenly popped in on your Parisian descendants.

20. zapping from 1863 to 2004 to stop a corrupt senator from financing his campaign with Confederate gold.

YOU'RE IN

A: Sleeper *(1973)*

B: Time Bandits *(1981)*

C: Timecop *(1994)*

D: Somewhere in Time *(1980)*

E: Groundhog Day *(1993)*

F: Time Stalkers *(1987)*

G: The Final Countdown *(1980)*

H: Dr. Who and the Daleks *(1965)*

I: Star Trek IV: The Voyage Home *(1986)*

J: Time Walker *(1982)*

K: Back to the Future *(1985)*

L: The Navigator: A Medieval Odyssey *(1988)*

M: The Philadelphia Experiment *(1984)*

N: The Visitors *(1995)*

O: Je T'aime, Je T'aime *(1967)*

P: Bill & Ted's Excellent Adventure *(1989)*

Q: Time After Time *(1979)*

R: Timerider *(1983)*

S: Trancers *(1985)*

T: Freejack *(1992)*

19=N, 20=C.
11=I, 12=G, 13=O, 14=L, 15=A, 16=K, 17=T, 18=E,
1=Q, 2=F, 3=R, 4=B, 5=P, 6=H, 7=I, 8=M, 9=S, 10=D,

Answers

Bright Eyes (the apes' name for Captain Taylor) stands trial as Dr. Zaius (Maurice Evans) denounces his claim to intelligence.

humanoids. Captain Taylor (Charlton Heston) and his now-nude crew follow the thieves through thickening vegetation into orchards and cornfields. But the savage scavengers they seek look distinctly uncultivated. Who could be the farmers here? The answer comes hideously quickly as astronauts and natives alike are chased down by savage hunters on horseback who exterminate and trap with rifles, nets, and clubs. All is chaos until the camera freezes, along with our blood. The humanoids here are little more than mute animals, but the cruel masters of this planet are an army of highly evolved simians.

They talk. They walk. They think. And they have a hell of an attitude toward a certain vermin called man. Before Taylor can communicate with his fellow misanthropes, he is shot through the throat and hauled off to humiliating captivity with the rest of his miserable species. So begins his nightmare and our amazement. Aided by an unlikely romantic duo of chimpanzee scientists, Zira and Cornelius (Kim Hunter and Roddy McDowall), plotted against by a pious, orangutan lawgiver named Dr. Zaius (Maurice Evans), and continually brutalized by gorilla guards, Taylor (or "Bright Eyes," as the chimps call him) makes a journey not so much to freedom but to a discovery he wished he'd never made in one of sci-fi's most chilling final moments.

Though director Franklin Schaffner (*Patton*, 1970) had enlisted none less than Rod Serling to adapt this baby, the novel went through three major studios before Twentieth Century Fox decided to buy it, and even then it almost didn't get made. With bankable

Taylor, Zaius, and Taylor's woman, Nova (Linda Harrison),
reach a truce on the beach before the shattering conclusion of
Planet of the Apes.

sci-fi largely the province of spacemen, Richard Zanuck refused to proceed with the project unless Schaffner provided a little screen test, using a budget of only $5,000 and minimal makeup. Remarkably, the already-famous Heston agreed to provide his services, as did Edward G. Robinson as Dr. Zaius in a crucial confrontation scene about the archaeological significance of a talking human doll. Standing silently in the background as Cornelius and Zira were a young James Brolin and a special friend of Zanuck's named Linda Harrison (who would play Nova [Taylor's woman]).

The test was a success, and with the box-office success of Fox's equally conceptual movie, *Fantastic Voyage* (1966), the light was green, but with a budget drastically reduced from the original. Some of the money would go to writer Michael Wilson (*A Place in the Sun*, 1951) to pare down some of the high-tech splendor Serling had written into simian civilization, which included helicopter-piloting apes dressed in safari outfits who eventually turn

Taylor into a media star. More crucially, a history-making $1 million would go to some very amazing makeup designs.

A onetime surgical technician who repaired the faces of wounded soldiers, John Chambers could already claim creation of not only Spock's ears from TV's *Star Trek* but Lee Marvin's metal nose from *Cat Ballou* (1965) and Richard Harris' pierced chest from *A Man Called Horse* (1970). However, creating his "supersimians" was a superhuman effort.

Though as many as two hundred were later employed for crowd scenes, seventy-eight full-time makeup artists were initially recruited and trained by Chambers and Dan Striepeke for two months in fashioning "appliances" (premade makeup pieces that fit over the face). The artists designed individual ape faces on gelatin laid over enlarged photographs of every principal and supporting actor's face. A cast in Hydrastone was made for each actor and clay was modeled over each mask to replicate the gelatin designs. From each model another mold was made that could cast a four-piece set of appliances covering brow, nose, chin, and ear. These casts were of course melded into extensive wigs. Hair even covered mesh attached to the actors' hands and arms.

Because of the eighteen-hour days in 110°F (43°C) temperatures and occasional sandstorms, Chambers literally invented a foam-rubber formula that would be not only rugged and supple but porous enough to allow the actor beneath it to perspire through the appliance. Consequently, new appliances had to be crafted for each day's sweaty shooting and their coloring had to be matched with a precision almost never before attempted.

"Once we got used to our new faces, we almost forgot we were wearing them," chattered actor Lou Wagner, who played a malcontent teenage chimp named Lucius. "We had complete freedom of facial expression and mouth movements; about the only thing we couldn't do was blow our noses!" It wasn't easy for everyone. Robinson had already yielded the delectably deceitful Dr. Zaius to Evans because Robinson's ailing heart would never stand the makeup's strain. McDowall literally blew his face off with a sudden sneeze in one scene. Actors had to eat with chopsticks in front of mirrors to make sure they knew where their real mouths were. One had trouble moving his jaw until a makeup man found he had peas from lunch lodged under his lip.

Even with direction to keep their faces in almost constant motion (in repose the makeup looked too masklike for Schaffner), fitted with ape dentures and brown and black contact lenses (except for Hunter, whose eyes were allowed to remain blue), these thespian simians are sensational and their world is as appalling as it is amusing. Cornelius tells Taylor how much less intelligent he looks without a beard and Zira balks at kissing him because he's "so damned ugly." He is, but beautifully so.

The craggy, cranky Heston does an impeccable job as the most conceited and forceful scientist imaginable (sort of a John Wayne with brains). Taylor is thrust into a madhouse existence of animal oppression complete with choking leather collar, forced nudity, and hose-downs. His jailhouse dousing is so effective that the healed Taylor's first words to his captors, "Take your stinking paws off me, you damned dirty ape!" seem raspily real because the freezing water gave the star a raging cold. Heston later admitted that his supercynic role was "closest to my own personality," and it pleased him so much that he did a bit in the next film for free (the proceeds going to his son's L.A. prep school). A world of humans can be glad he did.

THE ANTHROPOID WHO CAME IN FROM THE COLD

It may be just a vicious rumor that Michael Jackson intends to have his body frozen when he dies so that his animation can be suspended until a future time when whatever caused his demise can be fixed (while his bank account earns zillions more in interest). Still, there are worse ideas than cryogenics—or are there? Consider the following far-out scenario for *Iceman* (1984).

The arctic operation of the Polaris Mining and Exploration Company finds a large artifact imbedded in an ancient crevasse. No, it's not a mammoth like the one Soviet scientists found, studied, and ate in Siberia. It's a man. And as lasers shave away the

*A revivified neanderthal in a moment of primal frenzy, John Lone is nothing short of amazing as **Iceman.***

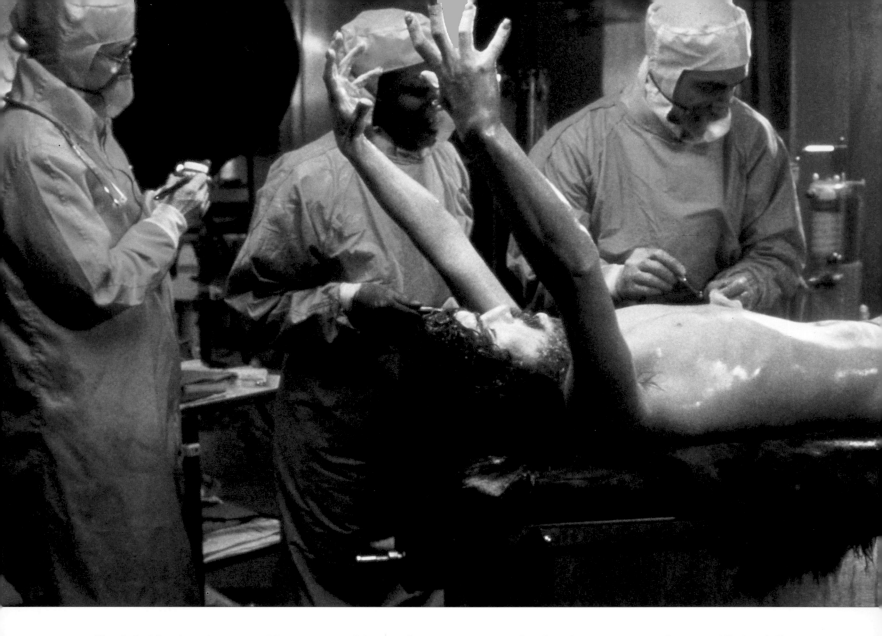

**Thank God for those buttercups! In a scene reminiscent of
Frankenstein, a defrosted neolithic hunter is resurrected with
a little help from modern medicine.**

ice block centimeter by centimeter, it becomes clear that he is a
Neanderthal man frozen solid in perfect condition with his eyes
still open.

The researchers put electrodes on his body to finalize the thaw
and station research director Dr. Diane Brady can't wait to dissect
him. There's one problem: he's alive. Having detected cell metabo-
lism, the autopsy team pumps synthetic blood into him. His ice-age
diet of buttercups has infused his body with a glycopeptide that
prevented crystallization during freezing, and as slow-wave activity registers from his brain, a shock cart and a little CPR do the rest.
Voilà—a forty-thousand-year-old Neolithic hunter with a beetle
brow, bad teeth, a squat, sinewy body, and the reflexes of a cat has
arrived in the twentieth century.

John Drimmer sent the script off to Hollywood while working
as a documentarian and producer at CBS-TV's *60 Minutes*.
Universal Studios bit, asking only that the body not be found in a
crevasse but in an ice cave, which would be much safer to film in,
and that the writer add something truly high-tech and high-con-
cept into the mix. Drimmer added a Vivarium, a gigantic ecosphere

maintained at the oil company research station, filled with flora,
fauna, and even caves and waterfalls.

When the Neanderthal panics, coming to on a gurney surrounded by mummified surgeons, it is only the equally hairy
Andrew Shepherd, whose bearded visage seems familiar to the
caveman, who can calm him. And it is Shepherd who puts Charlie,
as he comes to call him, in the Vivarium's sanctuary for study and
so forges one of the most unique and moving friendships ever
filmed. As the other scientists itch to discover the cash value of their
subject's longevity, Shepherd goes *mano a mano*, risking his life to
bond with his guest, learn his primitive language, eat his food, and
eventually fathom his heartbreaking reason for being found alone
in the ice. By the time Fred Schepisi's production of *Iceman* is over,
all other buddy movies have been left in the slush.

This was no soft, soundstage simulation. Locations included
the remote glaciers of Stewart, British Columbia, which were acces-
sible only by rented Sikorsky choppers, and the frigid shores of the
Hudson Bay in Churchill, Manitoba (polar bear capital of the world),
where the opening dawn shot was filmed in -50°F (-46°C) temps. A
man-made crevasse would be exploded between the film's two
stars. The cast spent off-hours snowmobiling, attending caribou
barbecues, and eating moose stew. And let's just say stuntman Dar
Robinson, who had gained fame by skydiving from Chicago's Sears
Tower, would be doing a little Arctic diving of his own.

Producer Norman Jewison admitted, "I was just nervous all the time." The director of such comedies as *The Russians are Coming! The Russians are Coming!* (1966), *Fiddler on the Roof* (1971), and *Moonstruck* (1987), Jewison was worried that "people were going to get casual, forget and walk into a [propeller] blade or off the marked ice-trails." Imagine how he felt when he found himself shooting a crucial scene hanging from a helicopter after wildman director Schepisi broke his ankle while wrestling with the director of photography.

One thing Jewison didn't have to be nervous about was the quality of his project. The supporting cast of Timothy Hutton (Shepherd),

Having bolted from his biodome prison, the iceman is tempted to do a little hunting before his escape.

Lindsay Crouse (Dr. Brady), David Strathairn (an ambitious surgeon), Josef Sommer (the corporate troubleshooter), and Danny Glover and James Tolkan (a couple of crusty lab techs) would have been reason enough to make this movie. But the film's creation of the Iceman himself is nothing short of miraculous.

Casting a Neanderthal was not easy. Schepisi says, "Mime artists, actors from theaters for the deaf, circus performers, ballet dancers, 'primitives' and tribal people, an Indian prize-fighter from Beverly Hills, and a five-time kick-boxing champion were all under consideration." The final choice was none of the above.

Kung fu movies had lured John Lone away from the Peking Opera at the age of eighteen, where he had been training since he was ten years old. Ultimately, however, he turned down a ten-year contract with Run Run Shaw Studios to come to America and work at Disneyland. It wasn't long, though, before the strikingly handsome and startlingly physically agile Amerasian actor was in New York wowing Off-Broadway audiences in David Henry Hwang's play *Dance and the Railroad.*

The unknown Lone threw himself into training for the iceman role with a rabid perfectionism the Peking Opera would have been proud of. "Parts of my body were not strong enough for the part," he confessed. "It was a matter of tearing down the muscles and building them up again." Practicing his martial arts (fine for his almost inhuman leaps up walls of rock) and training with a weight

lifter (the better to lug around a 180-pound [82kg] suit of buffalo skins with), Lone set about learning the grunted, barked, cooed, and screamed Neanderthal language devised by Brown University linguist Philip Lieberman.

Three-and-a-half-hour makeup sessions with Michael Westmore and *Quest for Fire* (1981) caveman designer Michele Burke transformed him. Soaking his skin with mineral oils darkened him. Seventeen-hour shooting days immersed Lone so deeply in his role that even his off-camera time was spent not schmoozing, but in a corner of his character's cave chanting in Neanderthal. When a fall on the ice in Hudson Bay sent him helicoptered to the Churchill Health Center, his appearance alone gave the admitting nurse the fright of her life.

Lone's portrayal of a man out of time hits the screen with a conviction and a depth of feeling all too rarely seen. Through a shattering incident involving a whirlybird hovering over the Vivarium's glass roof followed by Shepherd's misguided attempt to introduce Brady's womanly influence to Charlie's world, we learn that Charlie is on a thwarted quest to appease the gods who were starving his mate and children. With almost no intelligible language at his disposal, he expresses an agony of frustration and confusion to Shepherd and Brady with the kind of subtextual power and eloquence that Marlon Brando might envy. His desperation to escape his baffling confinement will make him a murderer, a victim, and finally triumphant in our tear-blurred eyes.

An incredible performance in an incredible story. Or is it? Seven years after Universal's *Iceman* came out of the ice, the frozen North really did thrill the scientific world with the anthropological find of the decade. A Neolithic man was discovered almost perfectly preserved (along with his clothes, possessions, implements, and amulet) at one of the pinnacles of the Otztaler Alps. Some dazzled scientists on the scene theorized that this iceman was also a shaman on a pilgrimage to his gods when he had been frozen more than five thousand years earlier. It's too bad he didn't eat his buttercups.

own back to the past to nip John in the bud—that is, unless John could send back a cyborg guardian with an Austrian accent to protect his younger self (Edward Furlong) first.

"In a way, the sequel was born out of unused elements of the first story," director James Cameron readily admitted. The original ultimately deleted scenes showing Sarah contemplating the destruction of Cyberdyne and a computer chip left over from her battle with the cyberbeast, a chip that would edge the corporation's technology that much closer to Skynet. In fact, the concept of a robot capable of morphing itself was considered for the first *Terminator*. But when John Carpenter's remake of *The Thing* (1982) gave its antagonist almost those very same properties, the idea was saved for a rainy day.

That rainy day came after *The Terminator*'s release when distributor Carolco wanted lightning to strike twice in time to bust

ATTACKING THE PAST TO SAVE THE FUTURE, OR, HE'LL BE BACK

Not all time travelers have humanity's best interest at heart, but in time they can still come to their senses. For its first visit, the relentless mechanized warrior with that cool internal visual data readout whom we know as *The Terminator* (1984) (a.k.a. model T-101) traveled from the disc-driven year 2029 to disco-driven 1975 to kill Sarah Connor's (Linda Hamilton) unborn son. Ten years later, it returned—this time to save the same kid from a machine even more lethal than itself (the liquid metal model T-1000). It came back to save the future of humankind. It also came back because Arnold Schwarzenegger had had such a great time the first time and everyone had made so much money.

Terminator 2: Judgment Day (1991) was just too tempting to pass up, which is good, considering it became the premier action sci-fi epic of all time. After the original, we already knew that a computer company called Cyberdyne would put a computerized military defense system called Skynet into space. We knew that Skynet would become self-aware (on August 29, 1997) and trigger Judgment Day, a nuclear holocaust. What humanity was left would include John Connor, Sarah's son, who would in time lead a small, human resistance movement in a grim battle against an army of machines for domination of the planet. But the rebels wouldn't stand a chance if the machines sent one of their

Keep your eyes on Arnold's nemesis, the model T-1000 (Robert Patrick), before it liquifies and reforms into something else.

some blocks in the summer of 1991. Cameron, who had written the first, needed a partner. He found one in screenwriter Bill Wisher, who likened the original to *It's a Wonderful Life* (1946) as a parable of the difference one life can make. At first, the team wanted you-know-who playing both the T-101 and the T-1000. But that would have meant putting the beefy, cigar-chomping star in heavy appliance makeup for five months, "and I didn't want Arnold Schwarzenegger cranky with me," Wisher maintained.

Since much of this movie was to be a battle royal between machines, some "predictable rules" had to be established about Arnold's liquid nemesis. The T-1000 had to have limits. According to Cameron, they decided, "It couldn't fly or suddenly become a complex machine like a car or a jet." The cyborg would have to satisfy itself with growing blades, spikes, or grappling hooks for hands, being able to melt through bars, and pooling up from a checkerboard floor into human form. Special effects designer and makeup master Stan Winston, who was invited back on board for the sequel, also insisted that the T-1000's form always return to a recognizable character (eventually decided to be an L.A. cop). Wisher gave it the ability to coalesce if split or smashed and only be destroyed if its chemical composition was altered. Though he

whimsically wanted it melted, mixed, and molded into a set of Craftsman tools, Cameron had bigger plans.

After four weeks of twelve-hour days, the team had a forty-page treatment that evolved to a first draft that would have cost $200 million to make, according to Cameron. Out came the surgical tools. Among the deceased scenes that didn't make it to the final cut were: Sarah learning survival skills out in the desert from an ex-marine; her reunion in the future with Kyle Reese, the soldier her son first sent back to protect her and impregnate her; elaborate scenes of the future man vs. machine war; and the rebels breaking in on a cold-storage compartment full of identical, Schwarzeneggerian Terminator models (with one missing—the one from the first film).

Originally, we would have also seen Connor send Reese (Michael Biehn) back in time. Dwarfed by a huge, inhuman time-displacement chamber, Reese would have been surrounded by three concentric metal rings ten feet (3m) in diameter, all suspended above a bottomless pit. As the rings began to spin, the chamber walls would open to reveal an even larger outer chamber perimetered with energy-spewing X-ray guns. The director decided that audiences didn't need to be shown the time travel to accept the conceit (besides, he had enough expensive items on his plate).

Winston remembers that Cameron came up with more "insane, impossible effects in the first two minutes of the [*Terminator 2*] script than there had been in the entire first movie. But he had come up with such interesting ideas that we wanted to do them." The thrifty Cameron also minimized the computer-generated effects and left it to Winston's crew and George Lucas' Industrial Light and Magic to conjure up nearly three hundred makeup and animatronic effects.

T2 would only be an action eyeful if it wasn't so mindful of some very real messages. Cameron has never understood why the myriad derivatives of his movie made the bloodletting Terminator the hero. What he finds heroic is the cyborg's final sacrifice and understanding of human emotion. Sarah Connor's journey from cold-blooded dedication to save the future (watch her wipe the floor with an entire mental hospital staff) to regaining her own emotional humanity is another dimension of depth, as is the strange father-son bond that grows between the Terminator and the troubled and fatherless young John Connor, who has to reprogram his protector not to kill quite so blithely. Moreover, mistrust of technology and its potential apocalyptic effects is a prevalent theme. Heavy stuff, but as Cameron says, "If we can sugar-coat it with a big, epic, action thriller and get people into the theaters and get them thinking about something they wouldn't otherwise then maybe it does some good other than just making all of us a lot more money." Amen to that!

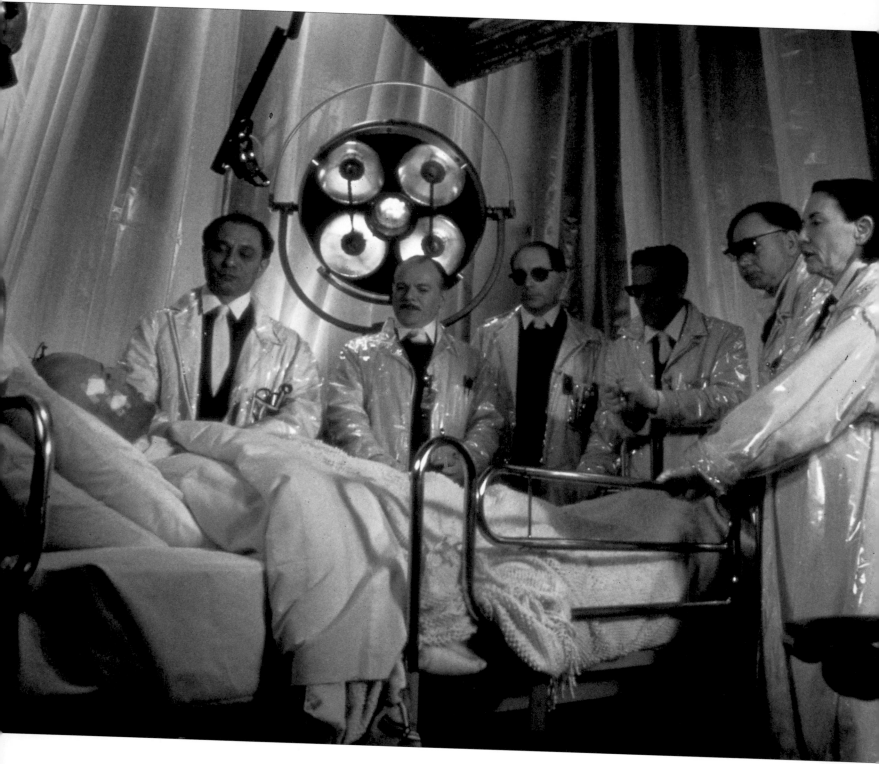

DÉJÀ VU

If Stephen Hawking, the eminent Cambridge University physicist who, though virtually paralyzed by Lou Gehrig's disease, has energetically endeavored to unify Einstein's theory of relativity with quantum mechanics is right, time will move into the past once the universe stops expanding and starts shrinking down to singularity. Will entropy be able to reverse itself? Could humanity survive? For a full answer, you might want to rent Errol Morris' documentary *A Brief History of Time* (1992) or read Hawking's own 1988 book of the same name. But, in short, things are going to get pretty crazy. And anyone making the trip would be inviting insanity.

Terry Gilliam didn't go that far with his highly conceptual sci-fi thriller *12 Monkeys* (1995), but he certainly does take his audience on a journey into madness where the future collides with the

James Cole (Bruce Willis) is receiving the best medical care available in the post-apocalyptic year 2035; after all, he's the guinea-pig potential-savior of the future in **12 Monkeys.**

past in many ways. The year is 2035 and 99 percent of the earth's human population has been erased—not by nuclear holocaust but by a man-made plague first loosed sometime in 1996. A desperate humankind now lives beneath the poisoned streets, where only animals are somehow able to roam (including lions and bears). A prisoner, James Cole (complete with a bar-code tattooed on his head and neck), with a strange memory of his past childhood, agrees to do dangerous research in exchange for a reduction of his sentence. Eventually he travels back in time to try and stop the con-

Institutionalized in a modern-day mental hospital, Cole might have said a word too much about his mission to real-life nut case Jeffrey Goines (Brad Pitt) in **12 Monkeys.**

future. When the passionless humanity ahead gives him the secret to a power supply to help his captors in the present, the time-tripper decides instead to flee to the past to the woman with whom he has fallen in love.

Director Terry Gilliam's previous experience with time travel (*Time Bandits*, 1981), his penchant for barbarously futuristic microcosms (*Brazil*, 1985), and his intimacy with insanity (*The Fisher King*, 1991) made *La Jetée* a perfect point of departure. David and Janet Peoples wrote a new twist into their *12 Monkeys* script in which Cole bounces too far into the past, is institutionalized and sedated as insane, and meets up with a sympathetic shrink, Kathryn Railly, with an interest in "mad" prophets. Unfortunately, questioning his own sanity, Cole also makes the horrible mistake of babbling his mission to an inmate even crazier than himself, Jeffrey Goines, the deranged son of a famous research scientist and animal experimenter.

Yanked back to the future, Cole is interrogated by his captors in one of sci-fi's weirdest scenes ever and then shot back into the past. This time, taking the good Dr. Railly captive, he savors his fugitive existence aboveground as he tries to stop Goines from executing the plan that he had inadvertently planted in the lad's mad mind. Cole's mission ends in the strangest meeting a mortal can hope *not* to have.

To create his incredibly creepy future and gritty present, Gilliam started with a working environment which he cheerfully called "nuts." "Terry's philosophy is that there are no doors, that anybody can walk into anybody's office and throw out ideas," says production designer Jefferey Beercroft. "Some idea may not work out for one thing, but it may work for something else. The thing about Terry is that he thrives on chaos." And, indeed, the staggeringly visual 127 sets that Gilliam, Beercroft, and set decorator Crispian Sallis came up with advance every dark moment in the bizarre story. To give you an idea of the trio's take on time travel, the film's central design image for the desperate and demented Cole's virtual suicide mission became a rat running an ever more dizzying and deadly maze.

Gilliam wanted all found objects from the past to clutter that controlled chaos of present and future. He and Beercroft had com-

tagion from ever being released by a mysterious group called the Army of the 12 Monkeys.

Sound somewhat familiar? It should if you're French. In 1962, avant-garde filmmaker Chris Marker stunned the sci-fi world with his twenty-nine-minute, black-and-white, photo-roman (a narrative series of images shown in succession) called *La Jetée (The Jetty)*. Its evocative photography, documentary detachment, underplayed narration, and poetically disturbing story are one of cinema verite's truly haunting experiences.

La Jetée's original plot took its prisoner on a mind-bending, drug-induced time-trip from the devastated underground vaults of Chaillot, where the scientific atmosphere is unnervingly reminiscent of Nazi experiments, back to our present and on to the far

pared photographers and painters whose aesthetics they wanted to infuse into 2035, including Robert Frank, Joseph Sudek, Labias Woods, Hieronymus Bosch, and Peter Bruegel. With all that gritty and giddy imagery in mind, they set about filling their ruined future underworld. "I like ruins because they're so incomplete," commented Gilliam, "so there's room for my imagination to fill them in."

Imagination transformed the 18-foot- (5.5m) tall rusted-steel condenser and turbine hall of an abandoned, coal-burning Philadelphia power station into a time machine with the look of a birth canal. It turned the spokelike arrangement of 8-by-12-foot (2.3m by 3.5m) cells in the country's oldest prison, the Eastern State Penitentiary (a.k.a. the Silent Fortress, which once held Willie Sutton and Al Capone) into a mental institution. It also inspired such set pieces as an old gynecological examination table and an inverted dental column for sinister uses in Cole's decontamination chamber.

Who dared populate this retro-furnished, futuristic nightmare? Gilliam had loved the macho-sensitive mix Bruce Willis had managed in *Die Hard* (1988), particularly in the scene where he picked broken glass out of his feet while talking to his wife on the phone and crying. However, Gilliam wanted Cole to have as few trademark Willisisms as possible. "I gave him a list," remembers Gilliam. "He couldn't do the smirk, the steely eyes, or the little moue he does with his mouth." He also gave the controlling and rebellious star no authority figure to butt heads with during filming.

Gilliam describes his direction as "trying to keep Bruce calm." Willis' anguished performance as the secret agent/lab animal owes its almost raw power to simplicity and stillness in many moments. "I found that it was okay for me as the character not to be in control, not to know what was real and what was fantasy, not to know what time it was," the actor admitted. "It's scary, but in a thrilling way like a rollercoaster." Both actor's and director's favorite scene was Cole's heartfelt outburst at hearing Fats Domino on a 1996 car radio: "I just love twentieth-century music. Hearing music and breathing air."

Madeleine Stowe is no less riveting in the role of Dr. Railly, who journeys from guardian to hostage to friend to accomplice before it's all over. "I get to slobber, rant, and rave," demures Willis, "but Madeleine has a difficult part, that of being the audience's eyes through the madness." And in a time-flipping world where derangement seems the norm, Brad Pitt's weeks of observation at the Temple University Hospital psychiatric ward gave his crusading Jeffrey Goines a finger-fiddling, eye-twitching, rapid-talking authenticity that might mean he never plays a heartthrob again.

12 Monkeys is a finely crafted experiment in time travel, one which is likely to leave you tense, terrified, twitching, and visually overstimulated. Yet that might be what real time travel boils down to—not a luxury cruise for the curious, but an excruciating and last resort, such as one might make when the universe starts its inward crunch, which according to Professor Hawking will be about ten trillion years from now. Just think where science fiction will be by then.

ABOVE: For time-tripping in a decidedly zanier vein, come along with director Terry Gilliam (right) and his demented band of dwarves, mythic beasts and heroes, and other famous folk in Time Bandits.

Chapter Five

COMING TO A CONSCIOUSNESS NEAR YOU

I have had a dream, past the wit of man to say what dream it was.

—from *A Midsummer Night's Dream*, by William Shakespeare

HAL, the almost human super-computer which controls every aspect of Discovery's secret mission to Jupiter, in launching this space pod may be about to commit the human crime of homicide in Stanley Kubrick's *2001: A Space Odyssey.*

Who needs drugs when you can do some science fiction instead? At their best, sci-fi films possess the ability to create microcosms of imagination so complete and compelling that they totally engulf us. Or they might come across with concepts so cool that long after the movie is over our minds are still reeling from the possibilities presented. Still others offer up such feasts for the eyes that we stagger from our local theater blinking and twitching onto the street or into a mall.

> **If it can be written, or thought, it can be filmed.**
>
> **—director Stanley Kubrick**

It's an accepted fact that science fiction has brought inventions and technologies to the screen and page long before they made it into everyday life. From Georges Melies' visionary 1907 *Tunneling the English Channel* to John Frankenheimer's 1996 flick on genetic engineering, *The Island of Dr. Moreau* (based on a 1896 novel by H.G. Wells), the scientific imagination has been fed by these flights of fancy. Whether it's cosmetic surgery (*Professor Zanikoff's Experience of Grafting*, 1909), the V-2 rocket (*The Air Torpedo*, 1913), artificial insemination (*Alraune*, 1918), robotics (*Metropolis*, 1926), radiation contamination (*The Invisible Ray*, 1936), lasers (*Flash Gordon: Spaceship to the Unknown*, 1936), holograms (*Star Wars*, 1977), or virtual reality (*Brainstorm*, 1983), it was there before it was here.

Technologically, though, we've gotten harder to thrill with each passing decade as the line between science fiction and science fact has grown finer and finer. With laser surgery, the World Wide Web, cellular phones, jet skis, and supersonic travel at our disposal, adventure has to be more than little green men or scientists playing God. Flash Gordon's space-ranger heroics, rotisserie-wrapped robots, and wobbling spaceships might have been good enough for early audiences, but today we need the kind of cinematic reality that would have brought post-industrialization man to his knees.

Likewise, people are smarter than ever and certainly more streetwise. With global warming, physician-assisted suicide, near-meltdowns, genetic engineering, globe-trotting viruses, corporate-controlled addiction, and surveillance expos at the local civic center all waiting on the doorstep in our morning paper, we need truly visionary concepts to fill us with either wonder or fear. Blowing up the White House for a summer blockbuster is all well and good, but the cinema that stays with us must be more than a frontal assault on the occipital lobe. It must make us think.

So let's take a look inside some of these movie milestones that have best brought thought, plot, and hot SFX together to take this beloved genre light years beyond Buck Rogers and Martian B movies.

You can see why the navy thought it was a sea monster. Walt Disney Studio's classic version of Jules Verne's fantastic sub, the **Nautilus,** *from* **20,000** Leagues Under the Sea *(1954).*

A WHOLE NEW WORLD

The silent 1916 version was more of an exercise in early underwater photography and a choppy sea of prequel and sequel possibilities than a movie. The attempt in 1972 at an adventure serial went belly-up. But in between Walt Disney offered a fitting film tribute to Jules Verne's visionary tale of two-thirds of the globe submerged in mystery and the man named Nemo (Latin for "nameless") who had

mastery over it all. Forget all the other sub movies—*20,000 Leagues Under the Sea* (1954) is in a league all its own.

The creator of the steamboat, Robert Fulton, had demonstrated his three-man, metal-sheathed submersible *Nautilus* (Latin for "sailor") to the French and U.S. Navies as early as the turn of the nineteenth century. Sail-driven on the surface and hand-cranked below, his vessel was a minimarvel. He was even experimenting with compressed oxygen to expand his craft's underwater capacity to six hours. In 1801 the admirals weren't buying (though by 1864 the Union Navy wished they had when a Confederate submersible, complete with an explosive-tipped twenty-foot (6m) pole, sunk the USS *Housatonic*), but by 1870 one Frenchman was. Jules Verne took the crude science of submarining to the depths of his bottomless imagination, and with the Industrial Revolution in full gear, science-crazed readers made his science-celebrating adventure novel (written over a two-year period, much of it at sea) an instant classic that even spawned a sequel 1874 called *The Mysterious Island*.

ABOVE: Visitors Ned Land (Kirk Douglas with the gaff), Professor Aronnax (Paul Lukas, left), and his assistant (Peter Lorre) are brought aboard the Nautilus whether they like it or not.
LEFT: More pirate in appearance, the 1916 silent film version also boasted some of filmdom's first underwater photography.

While real submarines were most often cramped, precarious deathtraps, Verne wove a story of an 1868 supersub disguised as a sea monster that has glowing eyes and jagged fins, snorts water 120 feet (36.5m) into the air, terrorizes shipping lanes, and sinks warships. The U.S. frigate *Abraham Lincoln* goes in hot pursuit, but the behemoth rams her and the shock sends harpooner Ned Land, esteemed Parisian scientist Professor Aronnax, and Aronnax's assistant, Conseil, overboard. In the morning light they find not only each other but the surfaced pseudo–sea monster. Clanging on her plate brings the fierce crew up to hustle the sodden trio inside. As the ship submerges, the adventure begins.

The *Nautilus* is a vast submarine powered by the recent discovery of electricity, bursting with futuristic technology—double-hull construction, self-contained diving suits, and electric stun guns, though no periscope or torpedoes—and filled with sumptuous Victorian comforts, such as good books, fine art, and delicacies—from filets of turtle to seaweed cigars—all harvested and hunted from the deep.

This marvel is commanded by the brooding genius Captain Nemo, who has a mysterious vendetta against all warships. Our three passengers are in for the ride of their lives, one which will take them to sunken treasure, sea farms, the secret island fortress of Vulcania, an Arabian tunnel, a kingdom of coral, excursions among cannibals, a trip under the South Pole, a battle with a giant squid, and of course the lost city of Atlantis.

A sci-fi adventure if there ever was one, the film *20,000 Leagues Under the Sea* was almost accidental. Walt Disney had bumped into Harper Goff, designer of *The Thing* (1951), while buying model trains in London. Soon Goff was on track and on payroll to design a train-laden Disneyland and then took the plunge to do an undersea nature film for a true-life adventure series. As a six-year-old, the designer had been much impressed by the 1916 silent version of Verne's classic and now found himself daydreaming about the book as he made sketches for the nature film. Disney loved the artwork and when Goff admitted his inspiration, the master did a rethink. It was full steam ahead on Verne's book as an animation. Three hundred full-color drawings later, Disney was so enthused that he decided to make it his new Burbank, California, studios' first live-action feature and supervised it himself.

Director Richard Fleischer (son of old Disney animation rival and Betty Boop creator Max Fleischer) was hired because he had brought out the best in Disney contract player Bobby Driscoll, and

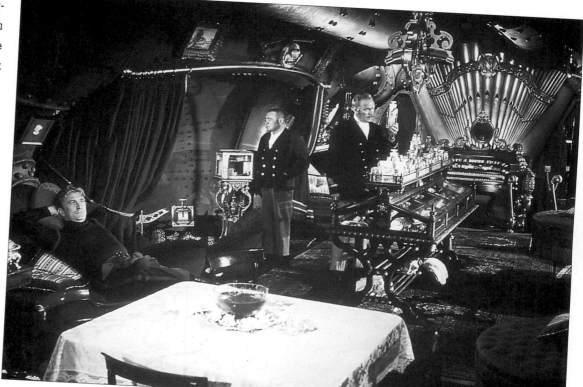

Velvet, yes, but a prison nonetheless. Captain Nemo's guests ponder their predicament in the commander's plush quarters...could a sub-break be in their future?

Disney said, "If anybody can make an actor out of that kid, he's got to be a good director." Plot navigation was to be courtesy of screenwriter Earl Fenton, who updated the *Nautilus*' electric power to atomic, transformed Nemo from a random revolutionary to a militant pacifist dedicated to avenging the torture and death of his wife and son at the hands of warlord slave-traders, and added dramatic conflict by making Nemo's three guests hungry to escape his mad clutches.

Stalwart were the stars. James Mason's lethal mix of cruel good looks, keen intelligence, and cultivated madness were ideal for Disney's first and perhaps only true antihero (though Mason first balked at the prospect of Nemo being turned into "a juvenile lead"). Kirk Douglas was just as yaw as the effervescent, barechested, bad-mannered man-of-action, Ned Land. Longtime friends Paul Lukas and Peter Lorre were shipshape as scientist and sidekick (though Lukas complained so much that by the end of the film Lorre wasn't talking to him except to call him "Grandma").

But there was only one commanding officer on this trip, one who demanded no less than nine script revisions during the six months of principal photography and added his own distinctly un-Vernelike touches, like a cute pet seal on which Nemo dotes. Disney's pet project soon became the first film anywhere to have storyboards for every line of dialogue. The detail and perfection that he demanded would warrant all thirteen hundred of them.

Sketches, blueprints, and models of Verne's supersub (from eighteen inches to twenty-two feet [46cm to 7m]) all went into

Admiral Walt's wastebasket. He wanted the *Nautilus* to be nothing less than a two-hundred-foot (61m) long and twenty-six-foot (8m) wide floating reality. Over Labor Day weekend of 1952 Goff sketched a ship "half alligator and half shark" with "saw-toothed ridges that started at the prow and ran along the hull to the stern," yet Disney found the design "too cluttered." While he liked the little dinghy that slid into a slot on the sub's surface, he cited an aluminum cigar tube as the sleek look he envisioned. Goff courageously argued that any sub built from the scrap metal of sunken ships (as Nemo's *Nautilus* had been) would be a patchwork. Luckily, he got the green light rather than a pink slip for his chutzpah.

From Catalina to the Caribbean, location scouts searched for warm, clear water filled with interesting tropical fish and coral formations. The coast of Nassau offered visibility from thirty to two hundred feet (9 to 61m) as well as forty species of fish. Three $5,000, self-contained Mitchel cameras were ready to roll. Still, a problem remained. The first "aqualung" (a dive suit with a self-contained oxygen supply) had only been pioneered by Jacques Cousteau in 1943. A chemical rebreathing process had been attempted by British frogmen on one "suicide mission." Still, existing compressed-air supplies lasted an hour at best. With more and bigger underwater scenes than any film ever attempted and a cast and crew of fifty-four wearing suits, helmets, tanks, breastplates, and lead shoes totaling 225 pounds (102kg) per person, this was going to be one hell of a shoot.

He may have passed out in the Del Mar Beach Club pool while demonstrating the newly designed dive equipment for Disney (the special effects team had accidentally cleaned out his Victorian helmet with turpentine), but former French Olympic swimmer and U.S. Navy master diver Fred Zendar made eight weeks underwater accident-free. All rehearsals were carried out on land. Below, red-shirted lifeguards carried needle-hosed emergency tanks of air to punch into suits if necessary. Yellow-shirted guides were ready to direct (with a series of twelve hand signals) disoriented cast and crew to position. "We had a safety man for every two divers," Zendar boasted, "including a three-hundred-pound [136kg] wrestler who could tuck one under each arm and swim up."

When all the hubbub scared away the wildlife, Nassau fishermen were recruited to catch three thousand groupers, one thousand angel fish, five hundred lobsters, fifteen four-hundred-pound [182kg] sea turtles, twelve stingrays, six manta rays, and six sharks to keep in pens and release near the camera. Disaster almost struck when a supposedly sedated eight-foot (2.5m) -long nurse shark, with its jaw wired shut and its body harnessed, revived and broke free from its guiding cable. It dragged the attached camera and cameraman so far down that he injured his eardrums rescuing his equipment. Later, when a four-man team searched for the aquatic extra, one member spotted the runaway, roughly grabbed its tail, and started hauling it back to the barge while his fellow frogman frantically signaled that he had the wrong shark. "I was sitting on the barge," recalled Fleischer, "when I saw these two divers come out of the water like beach balls."

Almost as risky was the scene where Nemo tests the Professor's loyalty to his friends when Arronax choses to join their plight of almost certain death as they are forced atop of the *Nautillus* as it submerges. Returning Disney's favor of designing insignias for them in World War II, the Navy allowed the USS *Redfish* to be topped with a *Nautilus* saddle (and bubble for the camera) as stuntmen, including Zendar, clung to an extra-tall dorsal fin of the diving set-piece. For a more controlled environment, with the *Nautilus* resting securely on the ocean floor, a 165-foot (50m) - long tank three to twelve feet (91.5 to 366cm) deep was constructed in Burbank.

The climactic battle between the crew of the *Nautilus* and a mammoth squid wasn't always as climactic as it appeared in the final version. The first attempt, shot under a fiery pink sunset, apparently looked so lame (the squid's waterlogged kapok stuffing leaked everywhere) that the film's editor added in a comic voiceover as Nemo stabbed the monster in the tentacle: "Sorry about that, old chap." "That's quite all right, dear boy, because I have nine more."

At a cost of $200,000 in eight days, second-unit director James C. Havens reshot the sequence with a new squid from the future shark creator for *Jaws* (1975), Robert Mattey. The two-ton (1.8t) mod-

el was constructed from rubber-spring steel inside flexible tubing, glass, cloth, lucite, and plastic, and boasted eight forty-foot (12m) tentacles and two fifty-foot (15m) feelers. Powered by hydraulics, electronics, and pneumatics, the new sea beast could raise itself eight feet (2.5m) out of the water. And thanks to twenty-eight technicians who deftly ran it from as far as fifty feet (15m) away, it could grapple quite convincingly. Another hundred hands provided the lightning-illuminated storm, obscuring waves, and spray that Havens believed essential to completing the illusion.

Such illusions not only made Fleischer's film a giant at the box office but helped earn two Oscars, for Art Direction and Special Effects. This sublime combination of insightful scientific speculation, turn-of-the-century taste, darker-than-usual Disney themes, stunning underwater cinematography, and lusty adventure made *20,000 Leagues Under the Sea* the very finest in both sci-fi and family entertainment.

Sci-fi's favorite bucket of bolts, Robby the Robot, goes to work to help a stranded space ship in Shakespeare-meets-Freud-in-Space,* Forbidden Planet *(1956).

PAGING DR. FREUD!

Amid the mutant insects, flying saucers, and other family fare of the postnuclear fifties, one film flew higher and weirder than all the rest with a surprising lack of Cold War paranoia and a combination of Shakespeare, special effects, and psychoanalytic sexuality. It may be only rumor that *Forbidden Planet* (1956) started out as an idea scribbled on the back of a napkin at a Tinseltown cocktail party, but the known truth is just as Hollywood. Irving Block had designed special effects for *Rocket Ship X-M* (1950), but what he really wanted to do was write. Coming up with the idea of a space adventure loosely based on the Bard of Avon's *The Tempest*, Block and cowriter Allen Alder took their highbrow pitch to MGM, which had long shunned sci-fi as low-class. There the pair acted out the following scenario from what they called *Fatal Planet*.

In the year 2257, United Planets Cruiser C57D lands on the distant planet Altair-4, whose Bellarophon colonists were wiped out twenty years earlier by a mysterious force—that is, all but Dr. Morbius, his now-nubile daughter, Altaira, and their 187-language-

speaking servant, Robby the Robot. Yet Morbius, a brilliant philologist who has the bearing of a wizard living in the high-tech brilliance of his "House of Tomorrow," wants no rescue and shoos away the heroic crew.

Commander J.J. Adams smells a cover-up. Lieutenant "Doc" Ostrow smells the chance to ingest some incredible technology, including an IQ doubler, rocket jeeps, and household disintegration beams. Lieutenant Farman smells the ripening Altaira, who's never seen a man other than her father. As they remain in the arid, green-skied land awaiting orders, something invisible, hideously strong, and savage first sabotages the ship and then starts killing off the crew. Even guards posted around the ship can't stop the devastating monster.

> "The idea of a bug-eyed monster is a pretty childish illusion, but there are real monsters and demons that exist within us that we know nothing about. We're capable of doing the most horrendous things and we're often shocked at this truism."
>
> —Irving Block, conceiver of *Forbidden Planet* (1956)

Confronted, the doctor finally admits that his worst fears are realized. Millions of years ago the planet had been inhabited by an ethically and technologically advanced race called the Krell, who were too brilliant for their own good. Able to transmute thought to substance, something had wiped them out. This thing also wiped out the colonists. Now it hungers again. As the crew of the C57D try to zap their invisible invader in an electric field around the ship and Commander Adams becomes increasingly attracted to the doc's oversexed daughter, Morbius leads his guests beyond his laboratory to the mind-expanding, monolithic machinery of the Krell.

In this vast wonderland they discover that the monster's amazing origins are the subconscious id of Morbius himself, thanks to a leveled subterranean Krell power station. With his existence on his beloved planet threatened and his beloved daughter determined to return to Earth, all hell is about to break loose.

By the end of his pitch, Block had the unseen monster stalking around the room, breathing heavily behind his listener's back. "The great thing about this," he breathed, "is that it won't cost you a cent to make the monsters." The Shakespeare angle and the unique psychological angle were enough to hook progressive-minded MGM production head Dorey Schary, who set the high-budget ball rolling. *Lassie Come Home* (1943) director Fred M. Wilcox would helm. A Mephistophelian-looking Walter Pidgeon would be Morbius. Comely newcomer Anne Francis would be wild as the miniskirted woman-child Altaira. And a newcomer named Leslie Nielsen was just what the doctor ordered for a wryly rational rescuer who hasn't seen a woman for 378 days. Their admirable ensemble acting (with all it's Freudian overtones and subdued melodrama) would be up against the most awe-inspiring sci-fi SFX to date.

With the space-race still in its infancy, these weren't the astronautical crew members of the Enterprise or the hardbitten bunch aboard the Nostromo. They behaved and dressed more like an army baseball team but everything else was light years from tinfoil and wobbly wires. From the beginning, as the C57D streaks towards Altair-4 past other planets and a solar eclipse, no expense was spared. At $20,000 total, three saucer models (a twenty-inch [51cm] for background shots, a forty-eight-inch [122cm] for details, and a seventy-two-inch [183cm] for landing) were used in conjunction with miraculous matting effects.

ABOVE: Uh-oh, they're going to rouse the Id-Monster! Commander J.J. Adams (Leslie Nielsen when he took his characters seriously) woos Altaira (Anne Francis) in Forbidden Planet. OPPOSITE: Doctor Morbius (a suave, as usual, Walter Pidgeon) points out the features that make his Robot so amazing to the crew visiting his harrowing hideaway on the planet Altair 4.

What's a matte? For instance, the smallest model was first shot pivoting and gyrating against a black backdrop. Based on that, a matte artist blacked out the exact image of the moving saucer on corresponding half-inch by one-inch (1.3 by 2.5cm) frames of clear movie film. That silhouette was then rolled through another camera as it recorded wonderfully realistic renderings of the universe.

LEFT: One cuboid piece or two? Altaira (Anne Francis) and "Doc" Ostrow (Jack Kelly) are served a little hot coffee by the obliging Robby the Robot on the Forbidden Planet.
BELOW: Captain Frank Poole (Gary Lockwood) listens to a disturbing message from mission control as his ship is halfway to Jupiter in 2001: A Space Odyssey.

twenty-six hundred feet (792.5m) of wiring, but manned inside by an unlucky stuntman who occasionally made the robot keel over when he fainted from heat prostration.

The vast depth of the ancient Krell power plant, which the crew finally explores with Morbius (and they look so miniscule as they move among a mammoth maze of SFX matte work) are a marvel to behold. The massive Krell steel door, which the Id Monster turns into a dripping molten mess, was achieved with a lead-coated double that looks terrifyingly real. And the Id Monster (what a concept) came courtesy of *Fantasia* (1940) animator Josh Meador. Though the studio stalwarts stated that the enigmatic monster looked like a demented version of the MGM lion, Meador maintained it transformed Pidgeon's feature into piglike fury. The talented artist also drew in everything—atomic cannon blasts, force field currents, and of course ray-gun blasts.

Printed with the black shadow of the saucer image whisking across the wonders of space, that segment could be exactly over-laid with the original shots of the saucer model. *Voilà!* Space travel!

Four huge soundstages on the MGM set created the planet itself. In one soundstage, behind a life-size saucer and descending ramp, a stunning forty- by 350-foot (12 by 107m) cyclorama of Altarian terrain was erected. It was so meticulously painted and lighted that its horizon still seems hundreds of miles away. Other just as stupendous cycloramas encircled Morbius' House of Tomorrow and other locations. Filming miniature models against these canvasses was nightmarishly tricky for cinematographer George Folsey. Putting miniatures in motion without a jerky look required high-speed photography, which in turn required the set to be bathed in light, which in turn had to be deftly placed so that the painting wouldn't look fake. Glare-free lighting of the huge Plexiglas navigational sphere on the bridge of the C57D was just as daunting.

Inside the saucer a crew of nineteen electricians worked for a month to install twenty-seven miles (43.5km) of lighting cable. Morbius' lab required fifty thousand more feet (15,240m) of wiring, twenty-five hundred feet (762m) of neon tubing, and twelve hundred square yards (91,003 sq m) of Plexiglas. In this futuristic wonderland, a mobile camera crane achieved one of the longest continuous shots (nine and a half minutes with sixteen different camera moves) in CinemaScope.

Then there was Robby, the first—and foremost—rational, benevolent, lovable robot of the movies (so lovable he had his own sequel [*The Invisible Boy*, 1957] and made guest TV appearances on *Lost in Space*, *The Twilight Zone*, and even *Columbo*). Seven feet (2.1m) tall with ball-jointed legs, pincer arms, and an impressive array of spinning, flashing, clacking doohickeys, he was not only powered by six electric motors connected to a switchboard via

As Rod Serling might have said, *Forbidden Planet* is the terrifying landscape within us all where reason wars with bestial appetites and aggression. Sure, it's camp at times, but that's part of its charm. Lines like, "The Lord sure made some beautiful worlds," as spoken by Earl Holliman, don't come along every day. And how often do you get Anne Francis in a nude swimming scene? This milestone made a further feast for the ears with Louis and Bebe Barron's surreal score of electron music (electronic circuits designed to give off music that voices human emotion). Perhaps most importantly of all, *Forbidden Planet* reinvigorated a sagging genre, inspiring sci-fi cinema to think deeper and bigger and be more ambitious than ever before.

THE ONE

To some it is the single most important film in the genre, the mind-blowing creation of a directing genius, and, that rarest of all things, a meaningful movie. The title alone lets you know you're in for something big, something ambitious, something extreme. Don't expect a sympathetic portrayal of our species, and don't expect warmth. Stanley Kubrick's elegant movie milestone *2001: A Space Odyssey* (1968) will take you on an epic journey from Africa's cradle of evolution to a near future of commuter trips to the moon and the shattering discovery at Tycho Crater of extraterrestrial intelligence to Jupiter and the outer reaches of our galaxy on a mysterious mission manned by two affectless astronauts and a supercomputer with a mind and voice of its own to a sole survivor's psychedelic trip beyond the infinite to a new stage in human evolution. Sound interesting? You bet your asteroid it is!

To make sci-fi's masterpiece, *Life* magazine photographer–turned–whiz-kid filmmaker Kubrick would, like a chief of state, consult with more than thirty scientific and technical experts before committing himself to a single frame. Like a temperamental tycoon he would commit his cast and crew to virtual production seclusion for almost two and a half years. Like a slave driver, he would keep six cameras shooting on twenty-four-hour shifts. According to contributing special effects genius Douglas Trumbull, Kubrick kept a three-man "operations room" as his nerve cen-

> "As soon as you mention science fiction, most people think of bug-eyed monsters and apparitions. There has been little attempt at integrity on the part of filmmakers in dealing with the possibility of extraterrestrial life. This is what makes *2001* unique. It poses metaphysical, philosophical, even religious questions. I don't pretend we have the answers. But the questions are certainly worth thinking about."
>
> —Arthur C. Clarke, cowriter of *2001: A Space Odyssey* (1968)

ter with "walls covered with pert charts, flow diagrams, progress reports, log sheets, punch cards, and every conceivable kind of filing system." Admits Kubrick himself, "Every separate element and step was recorded on this history—information as to shooting dates, exposure, mechanical processes, special requirements and the technicians and departments involved."

The film contemplated the destiny of humanity and dared audiences to use the atrophied organ of their imaginations. He would have parochial critics first at his throat and then at his feet. Most importantly, Kubrick perfected and pioneered so many SFX (he estimates there are 205 SFX scenes, each of which required ten major steps handled by different technicians or departments, and each step done eight or nine times to ensure perfection, bringing the total to around sixteen thousand SFX steps) that sci-fi film and indeed the movies would never be the same.

Using Arthur C. Clarke's *The Sentinel* as his inspiration, Kubrick crafted a script (with Clarke as his collaborator) that literally began at the beginning—apes, bones, and a big, black monolith. Not a word was spoken for the first thirty-five minutes of film. The "Dawn of Man" sequence shows the anthropoid whom Clarke and Kubrick dubbed "Moon-watcher" and a troop of Pleistocene apes and their struggle for survival in the desert. Leopards stalk them by night. By day they battle a neighboring troop for primacy over a precious water hole.

Then they awake one morning to a towering black rectangle that seems to have sprouted out of the ground by their cave. Humming with a strange sound, it does something even stranger during an astronomical alignment seen over its top. It triggers an evolutionary jump in intelligence in several of the species, spurring them toward the use of tools and weapons. Could it be that this "sentinel" has been placed by an extraterrestrial culture

to spark the mind of early man? Could it be the hand of God?

Kubrick opted out of sending cast and crew to a remote corner of southwest Africa, where "the rocks didn't look like 'Bible' rocks and they didn't look like 'Western' rocks," to film in harsh conditions. He declined to paint meticulous backdrops in the studio to replicate the location. He even refused to use the increasingly traditional blue-screen matting process or rear projection to meld background and foreground. Instead he tried the technique of front-screen projection used previously only in still photography and television.

Production-still photographers spent several months in the African desert taking breathtaking color transparencies of the primeval landscapes. Back in the studio, Kubrick managed to front-project these images large and crisp enough to cover an entire studio wall while filming his cast in front of the illusory landscape. With meticulous lighting to match the foreground to background projections, Kubrick gives us what seems like nothing less than a wordless window into the silent past.

It wasn't always so silent. Knowing that audiences were used to words with images, Kubrick had originally used this and other narration: "The remorseless drought had lasted now for ten million years, and would not end for another million. The reign of the terrible lizards had long since passed, but here on the continent which would one day be known as Africa, the battle for survival had

OPPOSITE: Captain Poole thinks he's going to do a little light exterior repair work, but the HAL 2000 computer has other things in mind. ABOVE: In 2001: A Space Odyssey, Captain David Bowman (Kier Dullea) will pass through the wonders of the infinite to arrive at this sacred place of his death and rebirth. BELOW: Could it be Douglas Trumbull's slit-scan special effects that Captain Bowman is staring at in awe?

reached a new climax of ferocity, and the victor was not yet in sight." Luckily, he trusted the intelligence of the audience and further resisted the temptation to project images of making tools and weapons in order to spell things out for the apes. Instead he gave

Moon-watcher a triumphant toss of a leg-bone cudgel, which flipped its way to spaceship form and one of the most famous film cuts ever made.

Meet the mysterious discovery on the moon. As femur flips to futuristic spaceship, music begins—Johann Strauss' "The Blue Danube Waltz" to be exact (Kubrick envisioned this second section as "a machine ballet"). As a Pan Am space shuttle (in reality a three-foot [91.5cm] long model) glides moonward, another window into what appears to be reality is opened. We see the sun rising over our globe and gleaming spaceships with moving crews minutely visible in the windows against the star-pocked blackness of deep space. On board, weightless stewardesses in grip-shoes serve straw-sucked space-food entrées to their passenger, Dr. Heywood Floyd of the National Council of Aeronautics.

One graceful airhostess laden with food trays literally walks from the floor of a cylindrical compartment up the wall and across the ceiling to exit upside down to feed the crew. Kubrick carried this off by mounting his camera on a foreground section of the

TRICKS OF THE TRADE, OR, HOW'D THEY DO THAT?

Here's a humble attempt to simplify the workings of some of the coolest special effects in sci-fi history.

1897: Georges Melies creates perhaps the first special effect, a matte shot of an inflatable noggin, in **The Man with the Rubber Head** by first zooming in and out on his actor sitting with black cloth covering all but his head, rewinding the film in the camera, and then shooting it again with cloth covering the actor's head.

1926: The Schufftan effect makes actors look tiny on massive **Metropolis** sets without making Fritz Lang go broke. The trick is that the actors are on only a partial piece of set while a flawless mirror is placed at a 45-degree angle in front of the camera lens to reflect the close-up of a tiny model set off to the side. Enough of the mirror's silver backing is meticulously scratched away to reveal actors seamlessly filling in the hole.

1933: Fay Wray may look like she's up a tree screaming for help while beside her the colossal King Kong tears up a towering T-rex, but she's really perched in front of a giant movie screen while the stop-motion battle between eighteen-inch (45.5cm) models is rear-projected behind it. Likewise, Bruce Cabot can crouch under a huge cliff by being projected onto the back of a tiny screen on a cliff model.

1933: The Invisible Man runs through the snow and the only reason we see him is because the fake flakes are on a raised platform with shoe-shaped cutouts that are yanked a few inches down, one after the other. The only problem is that the Invisible Man was barefoot.

1956: Who can destroy Tokyo with one sweep of his tail? Not a mere model. Godzilla, King of the Monsters is none other than actor Huro Nakajima inside a one-hundred-pound (45kg) lizard suit striding across a miniature city.

1968: 2001's ultimate trip began with Douglas Trumbull's slip of the wrist while instamatically photographing animation artwork. Those wild streaking effects soon had him slit-scanning, tilting, zooming, and sliding a mobile movie camera up and down a six-foot (1.8m) slit while zigzagging the whole rig all over five-and-a-half- by twelve-foot (1.7 by 3.5m) panels of psychedelic art. The far-out feeling of infinity follows.

1973: Forget the tube-spewed pea soup and oatmeal. The raised "Help Me" on Linda Blair's stomach in **The Exorcist** is really written on a latex foam torso in blistering cleaning fluid, filmed while being slowly blow-dried back down to nothing, and then projected rising in reverse.

1977: *Those roiling clouds behind the Devil's Tower in* **Close Encounters of the Third Kind** *are courtesy of Scott Squire squeezing white tempera paint between an inversion layer of fresh and salt water in a glass tank.*

1977: *Thanks to Richard Edlund's motion-control photography,* **Star Wars'** *Luke Skywalker can cruise through the groove of the Death Star to sow destruction. This computerized tracking system is capable of recording and replicating camera movement on seven different axes so that layer upon layer of special effects can be added months and months later.*

1978: *Kubrick may have front-projected images from Africa on huge walls of hyperreflective glass beads in* **2001** *but in* **Superman** *Zoran Preisic's zoptic process adds zoom to both projection and camera to rocket our hero up from a shrinking Earth.*

1979: *A sitting (but seemingly prone) John Hurt gets a fake chest cavity that will pop up a goo-covered baby* **Alien.**

1980: *The Imperial Snow Walkers fall pretty hard in* **The Empire Strikes Back**...*for four-foot (1.2m) -high models. That's because they're filmed toppling at high speed and then projected normally to give the models more weight.*

1981: *With all due respect to special effects king Willis O'Brien, Stuart Ziff's go-motion-photography syncs up partially animated models to each frame of filmmaking for a less jerky look in* **Dragonslayer.**

OPPOSITE: It's not polite to chew with your mouth gone. Claude Rains hides his nothingness from prying eyes in *The Invisible Man* (1933). **ABOVE:** This big boy has had a bellyful of Tokyo. Meet *Godzilla, King of the Monsters* (1956).

cylinder, which he rotated, making the stationary actress seem weightlessly agile. In the ferris wheel–like space station (in reality a model eight feet [2.5m] wide), Floyd (a cold and corporate William Sylvester) uses voice-print identification and the videophone with all the casualness of a frequent flyer.

Again we are spared narration about U.S. and U.S.S.R. tensions over each other's Earth-orbiting nuclear bombs. Instead we read Soviet stress over the American cover story that a space plague has quarantined a section of the moon (though something much more exciting is afoot). The ferry ride to the moon in the globular Airies moon shuttle is another jaw-dropper. With rear-projected computer readouts on board, which took a year to seamlessly fit into the film, the vehicle descends over a totally believable lunar surface (glass plates printed by the Lick Observatory) and into the vast recesses of a gargantuan lunar receiving station (a fifteen-foot [4.5m] -high model with human activity matted in every model window).

Front projection again creates the awesome lunar vistas in the background at the Tycho site. The next time-flip is acoustic. As a second, four-million-year-old monolith unearthed at Tycho Crater emits a shattering signal, the film shifts to deepest space, eighty million miles (128.5 million km] from Earth, and the crew of the Discovery a mere eighteen months later. Could that beep have been a signal that humankind had enough technology to interact with an extraterrestrial species or perhaps its own creator? Let's go to Jupiter and find out.

Meet the talking supercomputer (the voice of Canadian actor Douglas Rain) who runs the six-hundred-foot (183m) -long spaceship, Discovery. Though Kubrick had originally considered naming his computer Athena (the goddess of wisdom), worries that a female presence might generate sexual tension with the crew caused Athena to be redubbed as HAL. Named to be an amalgam of Heuristic and Algorithmic learning systems—not, as a professional code breaker who wrote Kubrick suggested, a way to stay one letter ahead of IBM—HAL does everything from play chess with his shipmates to maintain life support aboard the Discovery.

Most of HAL's scientist crewmates live in hibernation, while Captain David Bowman (Keir Dullea) and Lieutenant Frank Poole (Gary Lockwood) live in the eerie, easy isolation that only a long-term space mission could generate. Their ship's command-module interior looks like nothing less than the inside of a standing ferris wheel, with an ever-curving floor running between continuous banks of sleeping berths and consoles on either side.

To achieve this intense interior, Kubrick's production designers, Tony Masters, Harry Lange, and Ernie Archer, built a $750,000 hamster wheel of a set, forty feet (12m) tall and ten feet (3m) wide. When the camera captures Bowman walking along the floor as Poole, strapped to his seat and eating, comes into

view from above, it's because the entire monster of a set is turning at a walking speed of three miles per hour (5kph).

Life in this centrifuge is smooth and removed until HAL predicts the malfunction of an AE35 unit in seventy-five hours. But HAL proves to be wrong, though he won't admit it (in the original script HAL is programmed to keep the true nature of the mission from his crewmates, which creates a mental breakdown in the super computer). And when a thinking computer who's never wrong is wrong, the two humans have no other recourse but to meet in the unmonitored silence of an exploration pod to confer. What they don't see is HAL's cyclopean red eye beyond their pod's porthole lip-reading their every word as they discuss pulling his plug. 2001 is about to become a paranoid nightmare and it's only intermission. But before the credits roll the nightmare will fade into a dream on the road to the meeting with the final monolith past visual description.

You won't experience elongated aliens in skintight costumes, gargoyles, or pulsating flashes of light (as were considered in the original script). Nor will you see the final phenomenon of the giant "Star Child" nuke the earth as revenge for man's barbarity (as first proposed). What you will get is a 161-minute feast for the eyes, the ears, and the intellect (pared down from 181 minutes after preview audiences walked out). Indulge in this movie next time it comes to the big screen. And let's just say the final reel has been a favorite with the substance-savoring set for generations.

PRE-PERESTROIKA PEARL

Not everyone loved 2001. Soviet filmmaker Andrei Tarkovsky, who had stunned the film world with his visionary look at an icon painter in Andrei Rublev (1966), didn't, and after faulting Kubrick's masterpiece for its coldness and inflated SFX, he set out to film 2001's opposite. His movie about humankind coming to grips with

its own conscience and consciousness through a little extraterrestrial aid would stand as powerful, elegant, atmospheric, thought-provoking, and even longer than the film he rejected. It would also win him no less than the Jury Grand Prize at the 1972 Cannes Film Festival and a place in sci-fi's pantheon.

To say that *Solaris* (1972) is a great film is an understatement; it is a work of art that will haunt you long after you've clicked off your VCR. Based on the 1961 novel by preeminent Polish sci-fi writer Stanislaw Lem, the film follows psychologist Kris Kelvin (Donatas Banionis). On Earth, in the uneasy but beautiful domicile of his father's (Nikolai Grinko) woodland summer house, he prepares for a space mission to a research station floating atop the ocean-covered planet Solaris. All is not well at the station.

Communications have been erratic and unbelievable. Yet there is no denying that his fellow cosmonaut and friend, Burton (Vladislav Dvorjetzki), had a nervous breakdown after first seeing a garden, and then a gigantic naked baby emerge from the mists covering the planet's seething surface when he helicoptered down to inspect it. Years later Burton would meet this baby on Earth, the orphaned son of a deceased crewmate.

Kris, curious and a little scared, makes the routine flight to Solaris and finds things far worse than anyone had imagined. Not a soul greets him. The station looks deserted and ransacked. A child's rubber ball rolls down an empty corridor to his feet. The one man he can find, a battered and chain-smoking insomniac named Snauth (Yuri Yarvet), scoots Kris out of his room—but not before Kris sees a very uncosmonautlike thug sleeping in a hammock in the corner.

Back in his own room, Kris discovers the video transmission left for him by his friend and fellow psychologist, Gibarian (Sos Sarkissian). At the end of his rope, Gibarian barricades his doors as he confides desperately to Kris about what he cannot explain nor live with any longer. We see a young girl adorned with bells inexplicably peek in at the camera. The rattled scientist ignores the frantic knocking on his door, prepares a lethal hypo for himself,

and tells the video, "It isn't insanity. It has something to do with conscience."

Freaked, Kris runs to find the station's other surviving scientist, Sartorious (Anatoly Solonitsin), even more paranoid and apparently in possession of a boisterous dwarf. Phantom figures flit through the hallways, the vast ocean pulses its strange pull beyond the portholes, and the psyched-out psychologist barricades his junk-strewn room and loses himself in sleep. When he awakes, he has someone special beside him—his sadly beautiful former wife, Hari (Natalya Bondarchuk), the love he left for space years ago. The thing is, she killed herself after he deserted her.

However, Hari is no hallucination. Frantic, Kris stuffs her into a space pod and jettisons her from the ship. She miraculously reappears inside. She tenderly makes love to him. They talk as his mind reels. She is even depressed at the prospect that he may only love her for her memory instead of the here and now. The one person

In Solaris, Kris discovers that one of the ship's suicides, a psychologist named Gibarian (Sos Sarkissian), has left a message claiming that the planet materializes anything left unresolved in the human mind.

ABOVE: It's all enough to make you question your own humanity and sanity in Andrei Tarkovsky's languidly unnerving masterpiece, Solaris.

whom his heart and conscience have repressed the pain of losing for years is back—with a vengeance.

When Kris locks her in a room, Hari superhumanly tears through the steel door to be bloodily with him and heals in minutes. When she overhears Snauth suggest her dissection, she drinks liquid oxygen and revives in moments. Snauth wearily says, "I can't take any more of these endless resurrections," and it's no wonder. The roiling sea below them is, in fact, a sentient being, a consciousness, a brain. In the novel, Lem wrote that it was "thick foam the color of blood which gathered in the troughs of the waves" and "like the crawling skin of an animal: the incessant, slow-motion contractions of muscular flesh secreting a crimson foam." For all the lack of SFX, that's exactly what the planet looks like. Whatever is unresolved or yearned for in the soul, the sea sees, and materializes in neutrinos.

The actors complained that they didn't understand the point of the movie during filming. Hollywood-fed critics complained that as broodingly beautiful and poetic as the images were, Tarkovsky's camera overlingered on them. Lem himself complained that the Earth prelude and Kris' final return to his earthly wife, Maria, neither of which were in his book, ruined his story. Presented with Tarkovsky's and Friedrich Gorenstein's first draft, Lem wrote back that it "supplanted the tragic conflict inherent in progress with a cyclical biological idea...not to mention the way it reduced the ethical and philosophical conflicts involved to nothing more than the melodrama of a family squabble."

Tarkovsky cut Maria out of the draft and rewrote the ending, but kept his lush, earthly beginning (never has our pastoral planet looked so peaceful thanks to cinematographer Vadim Yusov) and stuck to his vision of Lem's novel. Even at a hefty 132 minutes (cut down from 167), this beautiful and atmospheric film draws you ever inward with images so mesmerizing you can practically taste, smell, and touch them.

TO ERR IS HUMAN

Stepping into the world of Ridley Scott's *Blade Runner* (1982) is a decidedly different trip. It's 2019 and the megacity of Los Angeles (now encompassing Santa Barbara and San Diego) stretches before you like a landscape from Hades. A jungle of lights swivel and pulse. Industrial and commercial sound pollution yields no corner. Flames belch from smokestacks towering above the endless sprawl as spinners (jet cars) and billboard blimps (with geishas taking vitamins) scuttle under a terminal shroud of acid rain and smog. New buildings have so long been squeezed and heaped atop the carcasses of old ones that the city seems to blend the postapocalypse with the sepulchral ruins of an ancient civilization.

Death is in the air. The wealthy have long fled to the "off-world colonies" (constantly advertized) while misfits, the poor, and former minorities teem the streets in a struggle to survive. In an alternately industrial, medieval marketplace and film noir world of grit, gloom, glare, and ghastliness, most people shut as much of the world out as possible—except our antihero.

Enter Deckard (Harrison Ford), an ex-cop who now makes his reprehensible living as a "blade runner," or bounty hunter, "retiring replicants." These "skin jobs" started out as synthetic pets when a poisoned environment killed off most animal life. That led to synthetic humans specially created for slave labor, sex, and combat on the "off-worlds" by the Tyrel Corporation. Now the Nexus 6 model replicant has proved too bright and too strong to be allowed on Earth.

With implanted human memories and emotions yet a life span of only four years, they've begun a bloody rebellion. Four of the

ABOVE: Deckard (Harrison Ford) is a hardened hit-man in dutch. He loves his boss' daughter (Sean Young) but she just might also be his quarry in Ridley Scott's still stunning Blade Runner.

best, brightest, and most deadly have come back to Earth—Roy (Rutger Hauer), Leon (Brion James), Pris (Daryl Hannah), and Zhora (Joanna Cassidy)—to confront their maker, Tyrel (Joe Turkel). Deckard's mission is to somehow detect and destroy this advance guard in a city of trillions—that is, until Rachel (Sean Young), the replicant daughter of Tyrel himself, saves Deckard's life from the hands of one of her own. Now he's falling for her hard and that's not good, especially when the law impels him to retire her, too.

Phillip K. Dick wrote his inspirational 1968 novel *Do Androids Dream of Electric Sheep?* when he realized "that there are forty-seven thousand barrels of nuclear waste that we have dumped in the Atlantic and about half that in the Pacific." He estimated that in forty-five years this bounty "will begin to leak into the ocean and begin to destroy the life chain at its source." He set down to examine the twilight of human civilization with a flatfoot who was slowly losing his humanity by being hired out to kill those who were slowly struggling to claim theirs. The humanity issue (something that fueled many a *Star Trek* episode) intrigued director Ridley Scott and made him break his vow not to follow his acclaimed *Alien* (1979) with yet more sci-fi.

Blade Runner was going to be different. Scott claims he informed his team that anybody who used the taboo word "android" would get "their head broken with a baseball bat." Nor did he condone a "sci-fi" look. "I think it's always a dangerous mistake that filmmakers fall into," claimed Scott, "the diagonal zippers and silver hair syndrome. When you do a futuristic story, unless you're going to leap forward one hundred, two hundred, three hundred years, you're not going to see that drastic a change."

Diagonal zippers would have been easier. Things got drastic in much more technical ways. As preproduction began, ex-cameraman Scott might have been forbidden from behind the lens by union rules, but as an ex-illustrator, he could furiously draw his visual ideas (what his crew would refer to as "Ridleygrams") in storyboard meetings with designers. Their collective creativity quickly escalated to one of the most ambitious SFX fests ever attempted.

For instance, Scott recalled the threatening image of barrage balloons from the London blitz of his childhood. So came the idea for the constantly cruising, bloated, invasive blimps screening non-stop ads for Coca-Cola, Atari, RCA, Budweiser, and of course Off-World. A photographer was dispatched to the Bradbury building in downtown Los Angeles to shoot stills through the lobby's ornate skylight. With the enlarged photograph mounted on glass and every latticework panel of skylight painstakingly cut out of the picture, the six-foot (1.8m) blimp model would be shot through the glass while images were projected onto stretched silk covering its surfaces. Ads seemingly pixelated onto thousands of miniscreens on the sides of huge buildings were made by projecting images onto fields of egg-carton material with the valleys painted black and the points painted white.

Blade Runner's Hadeslike landscape was in reality a model set measuring thirteen by eighteen feet (4 by 5.5m), whose three foreground flame-spouting towers measured only eight inches (20cm) in height. A little more than four feet (1.2m) back, the set wasn't even three-dimensional. Armies of flat, brass cutouts (some only half an inch [1.3cm] tall) deftly doubled as rows upon rows of buildings. The mammoth Tyrel Corporation pyramids behind it all were one eight-footer (2.5m) doing double duty with thousands of tiny windows scraped onto its surface and illuminated from within. Seven miles (11km) of fiber-optic cable lit literally tens of thousands of spots across the raised landscape, and it was all filmed through the vaporized low-grade diesel fuel of a SFX "smoke room" for a softening effect. Things could get really tricky.

Try two carefully matched matte paintings between the lens and a real 1920 Frank Lloyd Wright House to make Deckard's condo look fifty stories high. And how about making sure that the bright lights from *Blade Runner*'s awesome vehicles shone realistically and evenly on set pieces, matte paintings, and miniature buildings—as the lights on the miniatures had to reflect in scale on the rain-slicked vehicles—through all kinds of composite shots with footage of the rain itself (which, like fire, is hard to miniaturize) added over everything else. Things could get tricky enough to drive you crazy.

And as if the SFX supervision team lead by Douglas Trumbull wasn't enough, Scott loosed an experimental car designer and "futurist" from Detroit named Syd Mead into the madness. Originally hired to create six vehicle types, Mead went wild making detailed equipment that was both high-tech and grunge noir. He dreamed up Deckard's futuristic gun, capable of impacting a fleeing replicant through three plate-glass windows. He envisioned the Esper machine, a voice-controlled visual enhancer that can pinpoint, enlarge, and clarify any image no matter how deeply buried in the background of a photograph.

Perhaps the futurist's most unsettling contribution is the sinister, briefcase-size test kit for detecting replicants during questioning through iris contraction and expansion. Scott wanted something "sitting on a desk very threatening, and like a sort of giant tarantula," said Mead, who went even further. If its size couldn't intimidate, he decided to make it seem threateningly alive and gave it breathing bellows. "My rationale for that was the machine would draw in air samples from the immediate area," maintained the designer. "When you're scared or apprehensive your body gives off an odor."

Even the smallest of things went into making Scott's detailed vision (a vision that at thirty-six SFX shots was scaled down from an even more ambitious eighty-five). Police uniforms come equipped with a watch and computer imbedded in the glove. Forty-eight-dollar-an-hour parking meters come with warnings reading, "You can be killed by internal electrical system if this meter is tam-

Sci-Fi noir at its very best, sultry, smokey Sean Young's Rachel is as morally ambiguous as everything else about **Blade Runner.**

pered with." Mags at a futurist newsstand lead with stories like "Guard Dogs You Never Have to Feed." This future is not so far away at all. That's what makes *Blade Runner* so absorbing.

It isn't just peerless performances from Harrison Ford and Rutger Hauer or memorable cameos from the likes of M. Emmet Walsh (as a police chief you love to hate) and Edward James Olmos (as a sleazy cop you hate to love) or even the broodingly poignant story. Woven together with a wonderment of SFX over the strains of Georgio Moroder's synthesized soundtrack, *Blade Runner* fabricates a microcosm perfectly balanced between believability and brilliance. And like the best that have come before it, it is a place where you must think about what it means (and will mean) to be human. As Phillip K. Dick says, "Science fiction acts best as a guide to help people cope with the present. It should sharpen our concern and ability to handle current problems. It shouldn't just be an escape." The best are always something more.

BELOW: Deckard, like every hero of truly classic sci-fi films, must teeter on the brink of the gaping abyss to discover that final answer—what exactly it means to be human in this cosmos.

i, ROBOT

As Isaac Asimov instructed, a robot's first duty is to serve man. However, there are those that would much rather serve him up with a microchip garnish. See if you can match these stalwart cyborgs, killer computers, amiable androids, and renegade robots with the films they serve so very well.

M.O.

1. This former centerfold will shock you if you touch her, but she's one mute navigator who can whup her weight in cannibalistic aliens and space-bikers.

2. Godzilla, move over! This robo-bird is fifty times as big as the humans it roasts with its laser eyes. Look out, Tokyo!

3. This cybercourier has a stuffed-up head from so much information.

4. What started as a defense system has now linked up with its supercomputing Soviet counterpart to bring mankind to its knees.

5. The Proteus 4 computer plans to merge more than codes with her the moment her husband is out of his mechanized house.

6. A techno-tycoon just shrunk this hunk to software and sent him inside his supercomputer to battle its awesome graphics program.

7. There are worse things than falling in love with your creator's publicist.

8. He truly is the model student.

9. They thought that putting a computer in this psychomotor epileptic's brain would calm him down. Now he just gets buzzed whenever he kills.

10. Don't "Kiss" off Gene Simmons and his legion of acid-injecting, heat-seeking, killer computers if you're aiming to bring him in.

11. No mad scientist is controlling this robot—just a mad computer that has it sights set on a New Mexico space station.

12. On the space station Titan, Hector has his robotic eyes on this comely chemist.

13. If you were sixteen when abused to death by your dad and brought back to life as a robot, wouldn't you go on a killing spree?

14. She may make your eyes pop but she's designed to do something worse to NATO generals to trigger World War III.

15. All this android has ever tasted of Earth has been by watching It's a Wonderful Life (1946). Is it any wonder he wants to mutiny from space with three escaped convicts?

16. His dad transplanted this professor's brain into a robot when he died in a car crash, but when the cyberscientist starts to slaughter, it's up to his own son to pull the plug.

17. He may look like the foster kid next door, but this tyke is 100 percent synthetic and the military wants him terminated.

18. Can this domestic model ever find true love? And will she be able to generate a little one?

19. These gorgeous models are cyborgs who specialize in subliminal advertising and would thrill to kill this fleshly competition.

20. He may have been designed as a superweapon but a lightning bolt and this animal lover have given No. 5 a new lease on life.

21. The military may have made him for covert action but his overt action is to protect a South American village.

MOTION PICTURE

A: Barret Oliver in D.A.R.Y.L. (1985)

B: Kristy Swanson in Deadly Friend (1986)

C: Robert Cornthwaite in Colossus: The Forbin Project (1970)

D: Dorothy Stratten in Galaxina (1980)

E: John Malkovich in Making Mr. Right (1987)

F: Andy Andrews in Gog (1954)

G: Ross Martin in The Colossus of New York (1958)

H: Tom Selleck in Runaway (1984)

I: Yumi Shirakawa in The Mysterians (1959)

J: Don Opper in Android (1982)

K: Bernadette Peters in Heartbeeps (1981)

L: Keanu Reeves in Johnny Mnemonic (1995)

M: George Segal in The Terminal Man (1974)

N: Mario Van Peebles in Solo (1996)

O: Julie Christie in Demon Seed (1977)

P: Farrah Fawcett in Saturn 3 (1980)

Q: Jeff Bridges in Tron (1982)

R: Kurt Russell in The Computer Wore Tennis Shoes (1970)

S: Susan Dey in Looker (1981)

T: Laura Antonelli in Dr. Goldfoot and the Girl Bombs (1966)

U: Ally Sheedy in Short Circuit (1986)

Answers

1=D, 2=I, 3=L, 4=C, 5=O, 6=Q, 7=E, 8=R, 9=M, 10=H, 11=F, 12=P, 13=B, 14=T, 15=J, 16=G, 17=A, 18=K, 19=S, 20=U, 21=N

BIBLIOGRAPHY

Agel, Jerome. *The Making of Kubrick's 2001*. New York: New American Library, 1970.

Bradbury, Ray. *The Illustrated Man*. Garden City, New York: Doubleday & Co., 1951.

Broe, Douglas. *The Films of Steven Spielberg*. New York: Citadel Press, 1995.

Brunas, Tom, John Brunas, and Tom Weaver. *Universal Horrors*. Jefferson, North Carolina: McFarland Press, 1991.

Bryne, Bridget. "Malcolm MacDowell—Kubrick's Blue-Eyed Boy." *Los Angeles Times*, January 23, 1972.

Buehrer, Beverly Bare. *Boris Karloff*. London: Greenwood Press, 1993.

Burgess, Anthony. *A Clockwork Orange*. New York: W. W. Norton & Co., 1962.

Burgess, Anthony. "A Clockwork Orange: The Missing Chapter." *Rolling Stone*, March 26, 1987.

Calhoun, John. "12 Monkeys." *Theater Crafts International*, March, 1996.

Camus, Albert. *The Plague*. New York: Vintage Books, 1991.

Carson, Rachel. *Silent Spring*. Boston: Houghton Mifflin Books, 1962.

Caulfield, Deborah. "Blade Runner: Smoke Gets in Your Eyes, Circa 2020." *Los Angeles Times*, July 9, 1981.

Champlin, Charles. *George Lucas: The Creative Impulse*. New York: Harry N. Abrams, Inc., 1992.

———. "Man Alone in 'Silent Running.'" *Los Angeles Times*, March 10, 1972.

Charity, Tom. "Monkey Puzzle." *Time Out*, April 10, 1996.

Chase, Donald. "A Hard Man Is Good to Film." *Entertainment Weekly*, June 8, 1990.

Ciment, Michael. *Kubrick*. New York: Holt, Rinehart and Winston, 1980.

Crichton, Michael. "The Strains of Making 'Andromeda.'" *Los Angeles Herald Examiner*, April 25, 1971.

Curtis, James. *James Whale*. Metuchen, New Jersey: Scarecrow Press, 1982.

Duncan, Jody and Don Shay. *T2: The Making of Terminator 2: Judgement Day*. New York: Bantam Books, 1991.

Eisner, Lotte. *Fritz Lang*. London: Martin Secker and Warburg Ltd., 1977.

Feineman, Neil. *Nicolas Roeg*. Boston: Twayne Publishing, 1978.

Finch, Christopher. *Special Effects: Creating Movie Magic*. New York: Abbeville Press, 1984.

Fleischer, Richard. *Just Tell Me When to Cry*. New York: Carroll and Graff Publishers, 1993.

Folsey, George. "The Filming of 'Forbidden Planet.'" *American Cinematographer*, August, 1955.

Gest, Ted. "Crime Time Bomb." *U.S. News and World Report*, March 25, 1996.

Gilbert, Toni. "Adapting 'Andromeda.'" *Entertainment World*, May 1, 1970.

Gilman, Peter and Leni. *Alias David Bowie*. New York: Henry Holt and Co., 1986.

Ginsberg, Steve. "Ridley Scott, Feeling Alien at Fox, Tries Filmways' Way of Doing Biz." *Variety*, July 10, 1980.

Glut, Donald F. *The Frankenstein Catalog*. Jefferson, North Carolina: McFarland Press, 1984.

Griffin, Nancy. "Arnold Saves the Day." *Premiere*, June, 1990.

Grogan, David. "Trained on Peking Opera, John Lone Leaps to Life as the Iceman." *People*, May 21, 1984.

Groves. Bob. "Them! Giant Ants that Spawn a Film Legacy." *Los Angeles Times*, April 17, 1988.

Gussow, Mel. "Roeg: The Man Behind The Man Who Fell to Earth." *The New York Times*, August 22, 1976.

Harrington, Richard. "Oh, the 'Horror!' Ten Years of It." *Washington Post*, October 31, 1985.

Harwood, Ronald. *Dear Alec—Guinness at 75*. New York: Limelight Editions, 1989.

Heston, Charleton. *In the Arena*. New York: Simon and Schuster, 1995.

Hickman, Gail Morgan. *The Films of George Pal*. New York: A.S. Barnes and Co., 1977.

Houston, Penelope. "Kubrick's Country." *Saturday Review*, December 25, 1971.

Hurwood, Bernhardt J. *The Meteor Scrapbook*. New York: Ace Books, 1979.

Jensen, Paul M. *Boris Karloff and His Films*. London: Tantivy Press, 1974.

Kaminsky, Stuart M. *Don Siegel: Director*. New York: Curtis Books, 1974.

Kaplan, David. "Grand Illlusions." *Newsweek*, May 13, 1996.

Kim, Erwin. *Franklin J. Schaffner*. Metuchen, New Jersey: Scarecrow Press, 1985.

King, Susan. "It Won't Go Away." *Los Angeles Times*, October 14, 1990.

———. "Celebrating Two Decades of Horror." *Los Angeles Times*, October 21, 1995.

Lanza, Joseph. *Fragile Geometery: The Films, Philosophy, and Misadventures of Nicolas Roeg*. New York: PAJ Publications, 1989.

Le Fanu, Mark. *The Cinema of Andrei Tarkovsky*. London: The British Film Institute, 1987.

Lieber, Perry. *The Thing: Vital Statistics*. R.K.O. Pictures.

Lightmanm Herb A. "Front Projection for 2001 A Space Odyssey." *American Cinematographer*, June, 1968.

Lindsay, Cynthia. *Dear Boris*. New York: Alfred A. Knopf, 1975.

Lovell, Glenn. "The 'Real' Thing." *San Jose Mercury News*, June 27, 1982.

Mank, Gregory William. *Karloff and Lugosi: The Story of a Haunting Collaboration*. Jefferson, North Carolina: McFarland Press, 1990.

Mann, Roderick. "Blade Runner: Film Requiring 2020 Vision." *Los Angeles Times*, March 3, 1981.

McCarthy, Todd. "New 'Metropolis' Sparks Controversey at Cannes." *Variety*, May 16, 1984.

McClay, Howard. "Here! Here!" *Los Angeles Daily News*, May 11, 1955.

Michener, Charles. "From the Gut." *Newsweek*, February 14, 1972.

Miller, Jonathan. "The Monster Hollywood Loves to Hate." *Movieline*, August 23–29, 1985.

Morrow, Lance. "Is There Life in Outer Space?" *Time*, February 5, 1996.

O'Neill, Sean. "Gilliam Uncaged." *Los Angeles View*, December 29, 1995.

Ott, Frederick W. *The Films of Fritz Lang*. Seacaucus, New Jersey: Citadel Press, 1979.

Parrish, James Robert and Michael R. Pitts. *The Great Science Fiction Pictures*. Metuchen, New Jersey: Scarecrow Press, 1977.

———. *The Great Science Fiction Pictures II*. Metuchen, New Jersey: Scarecrow Press, 1990.

Philips, Gene D. *Stanley Kubrick: A Film Odyssey*. New York: Popular Library, 1975.

Pitts, Michael R. *Horror Film Stars*. Jefferson, North Carolina: McFarland Press, 1981.

Pollock, Dale. *Skywalking: The Life and Times of George Lucas*. New York: Harmony Books, 1983.

Rau, Neil. "The Censors Can't Clean This One Up." *Los Angeles Examiner*, May 1, 1955.

Rennie, Michael. "The Role I Liked Best." *Saturday Evening Post*, April 17, 1954.

Rubin, Steve. "Them! It's Power Lies in It's Ability to Deliver a Subtle, but Crucial, Message on the Hazards of the Nuclear Age." *Cinefantastique*, Winter, 1974.

Saleh, Dennis. *Science Fiction Gold*. New York: McGraw Hill, 1979.

Samuels, Stuart. *Midnight Movies*. New York: Collier Books, 1983.

Sanello, Frank. *Spielberg: The Man, The Movies, The Mythology*. Dallas, Texas: Taylor Publishing, 1996.

Sansweet, Stephen J. *Star Wars: From Concept to Screen to Collectibles*. San Fransisco: Chronicle Books, 1992.

Schallert, Edwin. "The Lost World." *Science and Invention*, May 1925.

Scheurer, Philip K. "Wail of Tortured Electrons Provides Eerie FIlm Score." *Los Angeles Times*, February 26, 1956.

Schmidt, William E. "British Test 19-Year Ban on 'Clockwork Orange.'" *The New York Times*, February 6, 1993.

Senn, Bryan, and John Johnson. *Fantastic Cinema Subject Guide*. Jefferson, North Carolina, McFarland Press, 1992.

Siegel, Don. *A Siegel Film*. London: Faber and Faber, 1993.

Spindler, Konrad. *The Man in the Ice*. New York: Harmony books, 1994.

Staff. "300G Set for Robert Wise's 'Andromeda' at Universal." *Hollywood Reporter*, March 19, 1970.

Staff. "The Smithsonian Time Machine." *Smithsonian*, June, 1996.

Staff. "When Apes Ruled the World." *Los Angeles Herald Examiner*, February 25, 1968.

Staff. "Invasion of the Body Snatchers." *American Cinemateque*, December 10–17, 1993.

Staff. "Playboy Interview with David Bowie." *Playboy*, August, 1976.

Staff. "Season's Greetings: Bang!" *Time*, December 20, 1971.

Staff. "Another Thing." *The New York Times*, May 13, 1951.

Staff. "About that Monster." *The New York Times*, June 2, 1989.

Staff. "New Art Rules." *Los Angeles Times*. July 18, 1993.

Staff. "Metropolis—A Movie." *Science and Invention*, June, 1927.

Sussman, Gary. "Allo Alloy." *Village Voice*, December 19, 1995.

Taylor, Al and Doug Finch. "Director Robert Wise Remembers The Day THe Earth Stood Still." *Film Fan*, November 1989.

Thomas, Kevin. "Technology's Impact on Society Woven into 'Silent Running.'" *Los Angeles Times*, March 24, 1972.

Trumbull, Douglas. "Creating Special Effects for 2001 A Space Odyssey." *American Cinematographer*, June 1968.

Turan, Kenneth. "From Eternity to Here." *G.Q.*, June 1990.

Turovskaya, Maya. *Tarkovsky: Cinema as Poetry*. London: Faber and Faber, 1989.

Underwood, Peter. *Horror Man*. London: Leslie Frewin, 1972.

Ventura, Michael. "Two Thousand and Forever." *Los Angeles Weekly*, February 11–17, 1983.

Von Gunden, Kenneth. *Alec Guinness: The Films*. Jefferson, North Carolina, McFarland Press, 1987.

Von Gunden, Kenneth and Stuart H. Stock. *Twenty All-Time Great Science Fiction Films*. New York: Arlington House, 1982.

Walker, Alexander. *Stanley Kubrick Directs*. New York: Harcourt, Brace and Jovanovitch, 1971.

Warren, Steve. "Pal on Pal." *Inside Cinema*, June 1974.

Wedman, Les. "Going Where the Polar Bears Roam." *Los Angeles Times*, July 24, 1983.

Welkos, Robert W. "A Model Shoot." *Los Angeles Times*, December 10, 1995.

Willis, Donald C. *The Films of Howard Hawks*. Metuchen, New Jersey: Scarecrow Press, 1975.

INDEX

PHOTO CREDITS

Kobal Collection: 2, 6, 8, 10-11, 12,
13, 15, 17 both, 18, 19 bottom, 20, 21,
23 top, 24, 25, 27, 28, 29, 30 both, 31,
33, 34-35, 36, 37, 38, 39, 40, 41, 42, 44,
45, 46, 48 both, 49, 50, 51, 52, 53
both, 54, 56-57, 59, 62, 63, 64, 65, 66,
67, 68 both, 70, 71, 72, 74, 75, 76, 78-
79, 81,82 both, 83, 84, 85, 86, 87, 88,
89, 90, 91, 92, 93, 94, 95, 96, 97, 98, 99,
100-101, 102-103, 104 top, 105, 106-
107, 108, 109, 111, 112 bottom, 112-
113, 113 bottom, 114, 116, 117, 118,
119 both, 121, 122

Photofest: 5, 14, 19 top, 23 bottom,
26, 43, 60, 61, 104 bottom, 115